LOVING AND LOSING YOU, AZAYLIA

LOVING AND LOSING YOU, AZAYLIA

MY INSPIRATIONAL DAUGHTER AND OUR UNBREAKABLE BOND

SAFIYYA VORAJEE

**EBURY
SPOTLIGHT**

3 5 7 9 10 8 6 4 2

Ebury Spotlight, an imprint of Ebury Publishing
20 Vauxhall Bridge Road
London SW1V 2SA

Ebury Spotlight is part of the Penguin Random House
group of companies whose addresses can be found at
global.penguinrandomhouse.com

First published by Ebury Spotlight in 2022

www.penguin.co.uk

A CIP catalogue record for this book is available from the British Library

ISBN 9781529149760

Printed and bound in Great Britain by Clays Ltd, Elcograf S.p.A.
Imported into the EEA by Penguin Random House Ireland,
Morrison Chambers, 32 Nassau Street, Dublin D02 YH68.

Penguin Random House is committed to a
sustainable future for our business, our readers
and our planet. This book is made from Forest
Stewardship Council® certified paper.

To Azaylia, my hero

PREFACE

When I was asked to write this book, I felt very honoured and blessed. It's a story of hope and finding strength, and if sharing my journey can help other people, I will be happy.

I felt anxious too, wondering how I would cope with retracing the steps of a journey no parent should ever have to take. But everything is about Azaylia now, not me. From the moment she was born, she changed my life and made my life, giving it the purpose and meaning I didn't even know was missing.

When my daughter became ill, I thought *I* was the one who would have to be strong for her. But Azaylia fought like the bravest little lion in the pride and I quickly realised *she* was the one who was giving me the strength to carry on.

My baby girl loved life – that was obvious to everyone who was lucky enough to meet her. And no matter what she was going through, Azaylia soldiered on with so much dignity and grace, giving the brightest smiles she possibly could. I tried my best to follow her lead and harness the positive energy she radiated every day. We laughed and we danced and we sang together, willing miracles to happen and dreams to come true, right up until the very end.

Now, however low I feel when I open my eyes in the morning and remember my daughter has passed, I ask myself: *What would Azaylia do?* In her short time on this earth, my baby handed me three powerful batons full of optimism, courage and love. I know I have to keep passing them on in her name. It's how Azaylia taught me to behave and it's the only way I can earn my place beside her in heaven.

Azaylia is a very hard act to follow. Her story lit up the world and her tiny feet have left giant footprints all around the globe. Through her charity, The Azaylia Foundation, I'm working to keep her light burning bright. We are raising awareness of children's cancers and fundraising to pay for research, equipment and to support children diagnosed with cancer, and their families too. I had so much to learn when Azaylia became ill, but no idea where to turn. If I can help other people in any way at all, I'll be so happy and thankful, and I will have done the job Azaylia prepared me to do.

I realise now that there were times during my daughter's illness when I was so scared and distraught my brain short-circuited. I didn't want to stare into the abyss and so I focused all my energies on Azaylia's immediate needs rather than on the big, black hole that was opening up before us. The tears are already running down my cheeks as I write this, but I'll do my best to sift through the darkness and bewilderment and fill in all the blanks I created in the bleakest of moments, and to share my story as honestly and openly as I can.

This is for you, my hero. I know you are looking down on me and I hope Mummy does you proud.

Let's go, champ! x

CHAPTER ONE

The pain is excruciating and I'm screaming in agony, completely taken aback at how sharp the contractions are.

"Gas and air! I need it, NOW PLEASE!"

I didn't think giving birth was going to be like this. Ashley had been so supportive during my pregnancy, even when I got tired and grumpy, moaning that I was so huge I couldn't even bend down to put my shoes on or complaining about the fact we were in lockdown, unable to go out and choose a pram or attend an antenatal class in person. In my mind's eye, our favourite, upbeat music would be playing during the birth, like Luther Vandross' 'Never Too Much' or Faith Evans' 'Love Like This', and Ashley would be rubbing my back and whispering soothing words in my ear as I dealt serenely with the pain. He'd kiss me tenderly, stroke my hair and tell me I was doing so well: 'You've got this, Safiyya,' he'd say. 'You're amazing, I'm so proud of you.'

It wasn't like that at all.

'Would you like an epidural?' the midwife asks, recognising that the gas and air are barely touching the sides of my pain.

I wasn't going to have an epidural, that was not in the plan at all.

'Er, can you have one ready, just in case?' I gasp.

I'm determined to get through this with as little intervention as possible. 'I'm going to try without first,' I say bravely, just as a huge contraction ripples through me and I scream in shock.

For weeks I've been asking friends and family how I'd know when I was in labour. 'You'll know!' they said with strange, secretive little smiles on their faces. 'You'll know!'

Azaylia was due six days earlier, on 4 August 2020. Ever since her due date, I'd become more impatient by the hour and was constantly trying to read my body for signs my labour was starting. I'm a detail person and I like everything to be neat and tidy and organised. I was adamant I wasn't going into hospital until the timing was just right and I wanted my admission to run like clockwork – 'I'm not going to be one of those people who leaves it too late and nearly gives birth in the car park,' I told Ashley. 'That's never gonna happen.' Equally, I wasn't going to be camped out at the hospital way too early, not least because of the current Covid rules. Like all partners, Ashley would only be allowed in for the bare minimum of time, so, if I got the timing wrong, I could be stuck in hospital on my own for hours or even days, which would be horrendous. And of course, it was unthinkable that Ashley would miss the birth. He *had* to be there.

As soon as I felt the first hint of a contraction I began using an app on my phone to monitor the minutes until the next one, so I knew exactly how I was progressing.

'Ashley!' I said excitedly, several hours later. 'It's time to go in now.'

I had this. *We* had this.

Ashley likes to be in control too. Dream, plan, then go and make it happen for yourself, exactly the way you want it to. That's how he has always operated, in all his different careers and in his life in general. I've taken a very different path to him, but I've also set targets and goals and made great things happen for myself. Having our daughter was the biggest dream of all, for both of us. This would be our greatest achievement, by a million miles, and nothing was being left to chance.

I had my hospital suitcase packed for weeks and I'd given Ashley detailed instructions on which nightie I wanted to wear when I gave birth and exactly what I wanted to change into afterwards – a black silk nightie with a long matching gown over the top. I had Azaylia's bag packed too, containing nappies, socks, bibs and vests. Her first outfit – a carefully chosen soft and snuggly white babygro – was folded neatly in a clearly marked see-through bag to make it easy for the midwife who would dress her immediately after she was born.

I expected I'd give birth that evening, within a few hours of arriving at our local maternity hospital. Why wouldn't I? The app had told me exactly where I was and I'd followed everything to the letter. It had all been going perfectly to plan, up until the point when I *really* started to understand what labour felt like. No amount of gas and air was helping, however much I dragged on the machine, and more pain and desperation were descending on me with every breath.

'We're going to have to break her waters,' I hear. There are voices all around me. Azaylia is lying in a breech position and we are spine to spine, someone says. I'm clawing at the sides of the bed with both hands, panting and feeling totally overwhelmed by the searing power of the contractions, which is intensifying by the minute. Somewhere amongst the fog of voices I can hear a midwife explaining that Azaylia's position in my womb is the reason I'm in so much pain.

'Oh my God!' I hear myself scream. 'Give me the epidural now, please!'

I feel the needle go into my lower back and wait for the agony to subside into numbness, but it doesn't. Eventually, I learn that epidurals don't work for everyone and, unfortunately, it looks like I'm in that minority category. Of course I am. The disappointment swamps me and I'm in free-fall now, engulfed in pain and despair and on the verge of losing the plot.

'Get back here!' I scream.

Ashley is trying to sit down in the chair beside my hospital bed and I don't want him to. Several hours have gone by – I have no idea how many. I want to hold on to him the whole time, to know he is right here with me. We started this journey together and we are staying side by side the whole way through.

'Give me more gas and air!' I demand.

'Safiyya, they don't want you to have any more gas and air,' Ashley says. 'It's not helping you right now. You need to have a pause and then you can have more.'

I'm not accepting it and I grab at the tube and try to drag some relief through it. It doesn't work, because the midwife has disconnected it, I find out.

I don't complain. I soldier on and Ashley is doing everything he can to help. He'd had a puff on the gas and air himself earlier, to lighten the mood and make me laugh. I think it helped to chill him out too, as he was jangling with adrenaline. I did manage to laugh at the time, but now I'm just gritting my teeth.

All I want is for our baby to arrive as quickly as possible. I want to see her face and I'm also excited to see Ashley's face the moment he becomes a daddy.

It was Ashley who first talked about us having a baby. Brought up in a large close-knit and very loving family, he was blessed with a heart full of love to give. 'Having a child is something I've looked forward to my whole life,' he told me very early on in our relationship. I remember the moment so well. I knew he meant every word of it and hearing him speak that way made me love him even more.

The two of us had been friends for years before we got together and the Ashley I knew was nothing like the person – or should I say 'persona' – other people might have seen on the TV. I wasn't with him when he was a professional footballer, living the high life, or when he did *Ex on the Beach* and earned the title 'bad boy of reality TV'. I had never even watched him on television and I didn't recognise the description. The Ashley I knew was never happier than when he was surrounded by his big extended family. He wanted to continue growing the beautiful circle his grandma and grandpa started, creating his own family and filling it with as much love and joy as he'd always known.

'I had to make sure I was with the right person before I became a father,' Ashley told me a little further down the line. 'And it had to be the right time in my life, when I could give everything to my child.'

He'd found the right person and the time was right, he told me. I'd never felt happier and I felt the same way, though my ideas about parenthood weren't exactly the same as Ashley's. Of course I wanted to be sure I was with the right person and that it was the right time in my life too, but whenever I thought about becoming a mum, I knew that above all else I would have to be sure that my child was going to be in a safe, stable and loving environment, and that, even if things did not work out for me and my child's father down the line, I would be in a position where I could look after them perfectly well on my own. Come what may, my child would always feel safe and comfortable, never afraid or neglected, confused or vulnerable. I was ready in myself and I'd found the man I trusted to be a good father, whatever life threw at us.

Me and Ashley had been together for a couple of years when we decided to try for a baby.

'Shall we?' He grinned. 'Shall we have a baby together?'

The conversation had been bubbling under for weeks, if not months. We'd been out for a lovely pasta dinner and had a few glasses of wine, and afterwards we cuddled up together on the sofa, feeling very happy and a little bit giddy, dreaming of our future.

'Yes!' I said.

It seemed a natural step for us, just as it seemed so natural to get together, finally, after so many years of being casual acquaintances and then friends. As kids and teenagers, we'd pass each other on the street in Nuneaton, giving a little nod of recognition because we'd seen each other around the town so many times. It never entered my head that I might one day have a relationship with Ashley. He was always a very good-looking boy, but he was three years younger than me, a gap that seemed *huge* when I was in my teens and early twenties. He was a lad's lad, too – a big, loud character who liked to party. That was all I really knew about him and that was the polar opposite of the steady, stable person I wanted as a partner.

'You're going to have a C-section.'

The midwife's words cut through the tangle of thoughts and torrents of pain I'd been immersed in for so many hours. It was early in the morning now and I was shaking like a leaf, every part of me trembling uncontrollably under my blue and white hospital gown. A soft voice from behind a mask was telling me that I needed to calm down. If I didn't stop trembling, I would have to be put to sleep for the C-section, and if I had a general anaesthetic, Ashley would not be allowed in to witness the birth.

Something shifted inside me when I heard that: 'Get Ashley here, now!' I yelled. 'Where is he?'

I don't know where I got the burst of energy from but I was screaming with all my might, my voice bouncing off the hard white walls.

I cannot deprive Ashley of seeing the birth of his first child. I can't let that happen. I have to calm down.

That thought was chasing round on a loop in my head, but my body wasn't listening to me. I was still shaking like a leaf and couldn't seem to stop myself, but I was determined to conquer this for Ashley's sake. If I had to have a C-section, I wanted a local anaesthetic – he *had* to be there to watch our daughter's arrival into the world.

Ashley came rushing towards my hospital bed: 'I'm here, babe,' he said.

As soon as I looked at his face it was like a switch was thrown. I stopped trembling, almost instantaneously, and then I told him I just wanted him here, by my side, every second, every step of the way.

'Azaylia is your baby too. You need to be here at the birth. We've just gone through all of this labour together, for hours and hours, and we need to stay together.'

I was so exhausted and just speaking to Ashley and focusing on keeping myself calm took all my strength and the very last drop of my energy. I remember being prepped for the C-section. I felt weirdly disconnected from my surroundings, even though the medics were setting up a little blue tent between my chest and my belly, and the doctors and nurses were talking to me and explaining what was happening.

All of a sudden, my body became a washing machine on full spin. It happened in a heartbeat, taking my breath away. *What was that? Has something gone wrong?* The sensation was horrendous and felt so alien to me, but almost as quickly as it started, everything stopped. The pain, the adrenaline and the nausea that had been sloshing and swirling around inside me – all of it disappeared, just like that. It was like stepping out into fresh snow, when everything is blindingly pure and white, and it's so silent you wonder if the world has stopped turning, just for a moment.

'Here she is.'

My baby girl was being held up in front of me. I looked at her face and the world was not just turning again, it was spinning like a top. *I'm a mum! This is my baby!* My heart felt like it doubled in size as it pumped out more love than I ever imagined it held.

Azaylia's skin was clear and incredibly fresh. She was flawless and absolutely beautiful. A midwife brought her close so I could give her soft cheek a little kiss. There was no blood, no goo – it was as if she'd come out of a bath of the most tranquil clear water.

'Cut the umbilical cord!' I suddenly yelled. 'Ashley, cut the cord!'

I surprised myself by screaming so loudly. It was as if Azaylia had powered me up – my tiny, perfect little girl had recharged me, with just one touch of her skin.

Ashley cut the cord and told Azaylia she was beautiful. I could see the love pouring out of him too. Our daughter *was* beautiful. I was marvelling at her beautiful eyes and rosebud lips and her cap of soft, light hair, and I was counting and re-counting her fingers and toes. The midwife performed the routine checks and Azaylia passed them all. The relief I felt when I heard that was incredible. Azaylia weighed 7lb 10oz, she had been born at 06.56am on 10 August 2020 and she was healthy – that was the most important thing of all.

'I'll see you soon, yeah? I love you both. You smashed it, Safiyya!'

It felt like I'd barely drawn breath after giving birth when Ashley was forced to say goodbye. We were out of lockdown but the Covid regulations were still very strict within the NHS and no family members were allowed onto the ward, not even the fathers. Ashley had been able to do the first nappy, because I was too sore to move after the C-section, but after that he was being shown the door as quickly and politely as possible.

Azaylia was in a little see-through crib now. She wasn't dressed in the babygro I wanted her in, but in the first thing the midwife had put her hands on when she reached into Azaylia's bag. I smiled to myself as I was wheeled onto the ward, arms held protectively in front of the half-numb scar on my belly. So much for my carefully labelled clothes bags and instructions about what my daughter should wear straight after she was born! So much for a natural, holistic birth without drugs or surgical intervention! But guess what? I didn't care that my well-laid plans had been thrown out the window, or that I'd have a scar on my belly forever more. All that mattered was that our daughter had arrived safely into the world and that she was healthy.

As I was manoeuvred into my bed I saw my notes on a clip-board. At the top were the words 'Mother – Safiyya Vorajee'. It might as well have been a Hollywood billboard, displaying my name up in lights, because seeing those three words gave me such a fantastic buzz.

I was a mother now, it was official! I was Azaylia's mum!

I had never been happier and my whole world had changed.

CHAPTER
TWO

'Hello, baby!' Ashley said, waving through my phone. 'I'm your daddy. I can't wait 'til I can kiss and hold you and get you home.'

Thanks to Covid, me and Azaylia were on our own in the hospital now, with not a single member of the family allowed onto the ward to visit. I FaceTimed Ashley as much as possible, but seeing each other through the screens of our phones was a bittersweet experience, as heartwarming as it was heartbreaking. Ashley grinned from ear to ear every time I pointed the camera at Azaylia, which melted my heart. It was fantastic to see the joy and light in his eyes, but I missed him the moment we hung up and I ached to get home so we could start being a family of three together. Ashley and Azaylia would never get this precious time back, but there was no point in dwelling on that.

'I can't wait for you to hold her in your arms again,' I said. 'It's going to be so amazing when we get home.'

I had already decided, long before Azaylia was born, that I was not going to be an over-protective mother in any way at all. I wanted me and Ashley to completely share the care of our daughter, just as we split every other aspect of our life 50:50. I wanted to share Azaylia with both of our families too. She was a gift to everyone and we would make sure she enjoyed the love of all her grandparents and aunties and uncles and nieces and nephews and cousins, just as we did.

Azaylia was sleeping soundly now. I lay there staring at her, listening to the sounds of other babies crying, other mothers talking on their phones, trollies being wheeled past and rubber shoes squishing along corridors.

Nurses came and went, but they were so covered in protective clothing I could barely tell them apart. Curtains were drawn around all the other beds on the ward to prevent the spread of any infection and there were signs and stickers everywhere, warning people to stay two metres apart. 'Wash your hands!' 'Wear your mask!' Black and yellow tape, like something you'd see at a crime scene, marked the boundaries of each bay on the ward.

Covid had affected me and all the other mothers on this ward in so many ways. Never in a million years had I imagined my first days of being a new mum would be like this. When I wasn't on my phone to Ashley or a member of the family I felt incredibly alone and isolated. I wondered if any of the other women were in as much pain as I was. Had anyone else had a caesarean? Did the other new mums have to lie there and watch the nurses change their baby's nappy because they were too sore to stand up? It would have been good to talk to someone who was in the same boat as me, but I never even saw another mother's face, and I didn't speak to any of the other women.

The nurses helped me to breastfeed, lifting Azaylia out of the cot and onto my chest at regular intervals. She took to it really well and I absorbed so much pleasure from feeding my daughter. It was a magical experience, despite the stabs of pain that rippled through my body, hitting me in waves as Azaylia suckled. Whenever it was time for the nurse to lift her back into her cot, I didn't want to let go. Azaylia's head smelled of sweet milk and I drank it in – it was like sinking into a warm bath, one I never wanted to get out of.

Azaylia settled easily after every feed and was no trouble at all. In the hours when she slept peacefully – and there were plenty of them – I had so much time to myself and more time to think than I could remember. Azaylia was a miracle, I thought. What a journey me and Ashley had been on. What a brilliant, wonderful journey and what a prize at the end of it.

• • •

'Will you grab us some Krispy Kremes?'

I remembered the day Ashley texted me to ask me that. It seemed like seconds ago, not years. He knew I was shopping in the Bullring in Birmingham because I'd posted something on my status on my BlackBerry. 'Sure,' I said, thinking nothing of it. There *was* nothing in it. Ours was an innocent friendship, one that had progressed from nods in the street to socialising with the circle of mutual friends we came to share in our twenties. There was a big WhatsApp group we were both in, where friends would take it in turns to suggest meeting at a café, going bowling or having a night out. *Shall we go there? Shall we do this?* Girls and lads, we all joined in, often ending up in shisha cafés together, sitting round a huge table, chilling out and having a laugh.

Being in this friendship circle was a huge breath of fresh air for me. I could see that so clearly, with the benefit of hindsight. I'd been in a really bad relationship in the past, one that stripped away my self-esteem, my self-respect and my self-confidence. I barely socialised – it wasn't worth the trouble it caused – and when I finally broke free, I had a lot of work to do on myself. I was very happy to be single while I healed and slowly started to grow back into my old self.

Ashley was always a great person to be around – the type of guy who lifted your spirits as soon as he smiled and said hello. He was upbeat and energetic and always up for a laugh. When I got to know him better, I began to see there was also a very genuine and sensitive person behind the party boy façade.

'You know what,' I told him, as our friendship started to develop. 'It's so good to be around nice people who are just being normal and kind to me.'

I surprised myself by feeling comfortable enough to talk to Ashley like this when we still didn't know each other that well. The relationship I had in the past had been violent and I told Ashley how I was threatened and physically and verbally assaulted, and how my car and house were smashed up.

He was shocked and it broke his heart to hear what I'd been through – 'I can't believe it,' he said. 'Your personality is so bubbly!'

'It is now,' I laughed.

Before too long, me and Ashley were doing things together, outside the group of friends. I was jumping on trains with him, travelling to pick up cars for a company he had at the time, or going with him to a club where he was DJing. One night I felt a bit anxious in one particular nightclub. Ashley noticed, which led to another conversation about my past. If I'd thought we might end up in a relationship together, I wouldn't have dreamed of talking about one of my exes so openly. It would probably have been a case of me saying, 'Oh yeah, I was in a bad relationship in the past' and leaving it at that. But we'd become good friends, were very comfortable in each other's company and were slowly, and naturally, getting to know each other even better.

I was surprised when Ashley started to tell me about periods in his life when he was depressed and anxious too. I knew his football career had ended because of injury when he was only twenty-two. That was years before we became good friends and I'd never considered how devastating it must have been for him, or how hard it would have been to lift himself up again.

Ashley told me that, after a string of injuries ended his time at Coventry City, he went out to play for one of the top Romanian teams, Gaz Metan Mediaş, to have one last shot at professional football.

'I can't imagine you out there on your own,' I said, thinking about the tight family circle he had around him in our hometown. 'How was it?'

'Quite nerve-wracking,' he admitted, forcing a smile. 'And that was before I got injured again.'

Ashley explained how he snapped his Achilles tendon in his first game in Romania. He'd already had two operations on the same ankle and there was no coming back, his career was over. He was forced to come home, he couldn't walk for twelve months and he spent most of that time on the sofa.

I could see the pain in his eyes when he revisited that part of his life.

'I went from having an amazing lifestyle with plenty of money to having no job, no income, nothing. I had bills to pay but I had no insurance, so I started to fall into debt. There were times when I was searching for change around my house to put petrol in my car, just to get from A to B.'

I was shocked and upset to hear that detail – I couldn't imagine Ashley in that situation. The Ashley I knew was at the top of his game. He was the guy who'd not only made a name for himself in reality TV, but had been DJing all over the world, was incredibly fit and upbeat, and had amassed thousands of followers on social media.

Something shifted after that. We'd dug another level into the already-strong foundations of our friendship, though I still didn't see the next level coming.

'I want to go and watch a film,' Ashley told me on WhatsApp. 'D'you wanna come?'

I hesitated before replying. No boundaries had ever been crossed in terms of our friendship becoming something more.

The cinema was a date-night type of thing, wasn't it? I didn't want our relationship to change and when I replied to his message I wanted to make that clear: 'Yeah, but we're just mates, right? We ain't going on a date here!'

'Yeah, yeah, cool, cool,' he answered. 'It's not a date.'

I wasn't entirely convinced by his response, so I deliberately wore a twin-set tracksuit and trainers and not the skinny jeans, heels and a top I'd have put on if I was going on a date. My hair would have been done properly too, instead of drawn into a casual ponytail.

After the film, when he pulled up on the drive at my mum's house, I darted out of the car pretty quick. 'See ya later!' I said, heading for the front door.

We still laugh about it now.

'You didn't want to give me a kiss, did you?'

'No, I really didn't!'

And I *really* didn't. I liked spending time with Ashley and I was enjoying his kindness and the attention he gave me, with no strings attached. It was obvious he was interested, but I was still finding my feet and regaining my confidence. Other guys were interested too, but I was happy being single and I didn't want to rush into a relationship with anyone.

As it turned out, my friendship with Ashley continued to blossom in the most natural way possible. It was like a rosebud opening up when the sun starts to shine and it happened so gradually and delicately I could barely see it unfold. It felt like one minute we were sitting in the car eating McDonald's – Ashley had quite a McDonald's addiction at the time – and chatting for hours as mates, to something much deeper. When I look back now, I can picture a speeded-up version of events, like one of those time-lapse videos on a nature documentary. Click! There I was, delivering doughnuts to his door. Click! There we are, laughing with our friends at the shisha café. Then it's just the two of us, as if the friends have peeled away and given us more air to breathe. Me and Ashley had an absolute beauty of a friendship that evolved into the most beautiful flower imaginable.

I didn't really realise how much he meant to me until one night when we talked about having food together and Ashley said he was doing something with his friends instead. I was disappointed, but then the next thing I knew, Ashley turned up at my mum's house. As soon as I saw him standing in the hallway there was no avoiding the truth.

There's something going on between us.

Ashley felt it too, but we both knew what a big deal it would be to turn our friendship into something more.

'You luuurve me!' he teased. He was testing the water, checking he wasn't going to overstep the mark if I wasn't feeling the same way.

'No, I don't,' I giggled, though I wasn't convincing anyone, I don't think.

We were in the car at McDonald's a few days later when I finally let him kiss me. He'd been making jokes again about the fact I fancied him and I was still being coy, saying I didn't. It so obviously wasn't ringing true and Ashley knew it for sure this time. It was only a casual kiss but it gave me butterflies in my stomach, something I hadn't felt for such a long time.

Oh my God, I want to live! I thought. I'd been plodding along in my life for such a long time, I realised, but that kiss changed everything.

. . .

A noise from Azaylia's cot startled me and, as soon as I looked over, I started to panic.

'Excuse me! Excuse me!'

My voice was getting louder and I felt frightened and tearful.

'Is there a nurse? Excuse me?'

Azaylia was being sick and I was trying to reach out and help her, but her cot was out of my reach. Stretching my arm out any further was impossible and I couldn't get up, because the pain from my scar was searing through me, burning me from the inside.

'Help me, please!'

Azaylia was lying on her back and she was going purple as her baby sick congealed around her mouth and nostrils.

A nurse arrived at my bedside. She was very calm as she turned Azaylia over and gave her a little smack on the back.

'It's just the first bit of sick, she's OK now,' she reassured me. 'I'll get her cleaned up.'

The roses were already back in Azaylia's cheeks, her breathing had returned to normal and her little eyes were dancing around, taking it all in. It took me a bit longer to recover, but that was fine. It wasn't about me now, it was all about my little girl. As long as she was OK, the world could keep on turning.

When I first told my mum I was pregnant she said something that has stuck with me: 'It's their shoes before your shoes,' she said, pointing out that I'd have to give up some of my luxuries when I became a mum. *I won't!* I thought. *I'll make sure we both have it all!* All through my adult life, if I wanted something, I went out and worked for it. If it was a new car, I'd look at my bank balance, realise I needed to earn more money and I'd go and get a better-paid job. That's how I'd always been. But guess what? I didn't want anything for myself any more. I was a mother and I had the most amazing daughter, and nothing else mattered.

We'd recently moved into a new house on an estate in Nuneaton, close to all our relatives. I wanted to completely redecorate before I had Azaylia but there wasn't time to do everything. We painted the walls and ceilings downstairs and had a new floor laid to freshen everything up, but the main priority was Azaylia's bedroom. I wanted it to be pure and angelic and clean and organised. During my pregnancy I worked hard, painting the walls white and spending hours online buying pink and grey accessories. Even Azaylia's toybox matched the décor, because I had it covered in shimmery grey velvet and studded with her name.

Mrs Hinch's tips helped me no end. I had drawers and boxes for everything – frilly socks, non-frilly socks, bibs folded in triangles, blankets arranged according to colour and texture. Azaylia's bedroom was like a well-stocked shop. I filled the wardrobe with clothes from newborn all the way up to twelve months, and they were hung on little baby coat hangers in age order. Twelve months – it would be the height of summer then and I couldn't wait to dress her up in all the pretty little outfits I'd bought.

We'd been on the ward for two long days when a nurse finally told me we could go home. My heart leapt and a huge smile stretched across my face: 'We're going to see Daddy and all the family,' I whispered to Azaylia, even though she was sleeping. 'Aren't we lucky? How amazing is that? We are all going to be at home together, and you can see your new bedroom and all the pretty clothes I've got waiting for you.'

She blew a little bubble in her sleep and it popped and dissolved on her lips. I'd never seen anything so mesmerising in all my life. Who needs diamonds and sparkling baubles? Azaylia was the most precious jewel I'd ever seen – I couldn't believe this perfect little girl was mine.

CHAPTER
THREE

I t took me a full six hours to get myself ready to leave the hospital. The ward was short-staffed because of Covid so there were no nurses available to help. It was understandable – rules were rules – but I was still in a huge amount of pain and the simple task of washing and dressing myself was like a five-act drama in slow motion. Every time I moved it felt like electric shocks were pulsing through my body and putting one foot in front of the other sent pains shooting from my toes to my temple.

How can I pick up those socks without rupturing myself? Oh no! I need to go back into that bag because Azaylia's bib is in there. I can't do it again!

After spending two days in bed, with nurses helping me as best they could, I was shocked at how difficult it was to do such simple jobs all on my own. Recovering from the caesarean would take twelve weeks, they told me. Twelve weeks! I'd have to take it easy, let Ashley do all the lifting, and I couldn't drive for six weeks. I'd already gone through being pregnant in a lockdown and having a baby during the pandemic, and now this. It wasn't what I'd have wished for, but so what? Azaylia was here and her presence overshadowed everything else.

My mum drove us home from hospital, and when we pulled up on the drive I saw a big shiny banner outside the house announcing 'baby girl!' It was a brilliant surprise. This was a moment I'd dreamed of and here we were, living out our dream at last – one little, happy family.

The living room was filled with pink and white balloons and there were Minnie Mouse helium balloons bobbing on the ceiling. My mum had done it all for us and I was so touched she'd gone to so much trouble.

'This is amazing!' I said. 'I love it all! Thank you so much!'

We posed for a photo in the living room, the three of us surrounded by all the glittery decorations and balloons. It's such a happy picture, one I'll always treasure.

'Daddy and daughter love you,' Ashley wrote on his Instagram, sharing the photo. He had hundreds of thousands of followers who started posting up comments and sending congratulations. I felt completely surrounded by love.

As soon as we got home, all the family were desperate to come and meet Azaylia. We were out of lockdown at last, but the latest Covid rules still meant we had to limit how many people were in the house at one time. The result was we had small groups of visitors instead of one big gathering, which made the celebrations last longer. I enjoyed every minute, even though I found it quite overwhelming to see so many family members in the flesh after so many months of restrictions. There was my brother Danny, my mum, my aunties, my cousin Chloe and all of Ashley's family. Their reaction to Azaylia was unanimous – everybody was totally blown away by her. They all commented on how beautiful she was and I could see the love pouring out of them. This baby was going to be so cherished, so safe, so secure. I was brimming with pride and gratitude.

'How are you doing?' Danny asked. He looked me in the eye, because when my brother asks me how I am, it's always a real question.

'Honestly, I feel like I've finally grown up,' I found myself saying. 'I'm a proper adult now. I'm a woman! I've got responsibilities and, from now on, my needs come second. D'you know what I mean?'

Danny knew exactly what I meant, and not just because he's daddy to my four-year-old nephew, Noah.

When our parents split up, Danny was twelve and I was eight. Mum went out to work in a fast-food takeaway and she and her sister, Auntie Hazel, put on discos in the evenings to make ends meet. Danny really stepped up as a big brother, always making sure I was OK and taking responsibility for me and my cousin when Mum and my auntie did the discos. Me, Danny and Mum did a paper round together for a while. It was so we could afford to pay for Sky and watch all the cartoons on Nickelodeon like we used to before our parents separated. I can remember that I was always frightened to get in the lift in one of the big blocks of flats we delivered to, especially if it was dark. Mum and Danny would both go with me on the stairs, with Danny holding my hand and telling me he was there and not to worry. Me and Danny always stayed very close and I looked up to him and admired him so much. If Azaylia and her cousin Noah could have a bond like mine and Danny's I'd be so delighted, I thought.

'Imagine when she's big enough to play with Noah and all her other cousins,' I said. 'I just can't wait.'

Danny was beaming. 'D'you think she'll grow up to be as cheeky and loud as you were? Poor Noah, he'll be given a run for his money!'

'Oi!' I said, telling my brother that if I wasn't recovering from an operation, I'd have whacked him with a cushion.

I was wiped out when all the visitors left. Ashley was amazing, helping to get me into bed and doing absolutely everything for Azaylia. I was so proud of him. Azaylia was like a delicate little doll in his huge arms and he carried her as if she was made of fine porcelain. I could tell he was worried about picking her up, let alone giving her a bath. But he did it all, with a big grin on his face.

'Goodnight, baby, we love you, Azaylia!' he told her when he finally put her down for the night. She was lying quietly in a Next2Me crib beside our bed and we both watched her drift off to sleep.

'Is she smiling already?' Ashley said. 'Look at her lips!'

'Probably wind,' I laughed. 'But it really does look like a big, happy grin, doesn't it?'

She was far too young to give proper smiles, but even so I'd never seen such a contented-looking baby.

Ashley got into bed beside me and we put on a film with the sound turned down low. This was our first night together as a family of three and there was so much love in the room I felt like I could reach out and touch it. This is what we had prayed for and wanted for so long. We both felt it; there was no need to say it out loud.

But my attention wasn't on the film at all. My mind felt blown and it was slowly dawning on me how much I had to think about and learn now I was home. For starters, I had to get to grips with the steriliser and the breast pump, and I was asking myself how I was ever going to get out of the house with a baby who needed feeding and changing every few hours. But I wasn't daunted by all my new responsibilities, it was the opposite: *Let's do this!* I was thinking. *We're gonna have the best time together!*

I could hardly believe how much my life had changed in the past nine months. The day I found out I was pregnant seemed a lifetime ago, even though I remembered every detail like it was yesterday.

'I think you should do a pregnancy test,' Ashley had said, when he called me at work. I'd been on my feet all day with clients. I'd told Ashley I was feeling tired, and all week I'd been coming home, flopping on the beanbag in the lounge and falling straight asleep.

'Nah!' I laughed. 'I'm not pregnant. It's winter-time, I'm feeling rundown. I'm just tired, I've been working hard and training a lot in the gym.'

All of this was true. As well as working as an aesthetic practitioner, I was building up a cosmetics company, Mz Pretty, which I promoted on Instagram. Things were going well and I was enjoying sharing posts and seeing my followers slowly build, though of course that was something else to fit into the day.

Ashley wasn't giving up about the test: 'Pick one up on your way home. I have a feeling.'

I reluctantly agreed, even though I didn't believe for one minute I was pregnant. After lots of conversations about having a baby together, we'd finally decided to go for it. I came off the Pill, we both started to take Pregnacare tablets and I was using the Flow app to log my periods and see when I was ovulating. We had everything covered, but guess what? Nothing happened, for month after month after month. We spoke to a doctor eventually, who told us not to worry. It was normal not to fall pregnant straight away, he said, advising us it could take a year or more.

What? I thought. I grew up believing I'd fall pregnant immediately if ever I didn't use contraception – I've been conned!

Ashley decided to take himself off to be tested, but there was no problem there. We simply had to be patient and stay chilled, that was all. We looked into going private, so I could get checked over sooner rather than later if we wanted to go down that route. There's so much help available these days, and so many avenues to explore, I reasoned. It could be something very simple that was stopping me conceiving. I made an appointment at a clinic for a couple of months' time just so we had the option there if we needed it.

Honestly! I thought as I went to buy the pregnancy test. *Why am I doing this?*

As I took it off the shelf in the local Co-op, I suddenly felt a bit embarrassed. I slipped it under the packets of rice and chicken pieces I was buying for our dinner that night and when I handed my basket in at the till I avoided making eye contact with the cashier. As soon as I got home I went into the bathroom, did the test and left it on the side while I went to get changed.

'Can I see the results first?' Ashley asked.

'Yeah!' I said, because I was totally convinced there would be nothing to see. My period was very slightly late, but we were talking days not weeks. I wasn't pregnant, so Ashley was very welcome to go and check the test first.

He waited a minute or two and then walked into the bathroom. A split second later, he walked out again with a huge grin on his face.

'Yeah!' he said.

'No, I'm not!'

'Yes, Safiyya, you are!'

He showed me the pregnancy stick and I looked at it in disbelief, staring at the blue line and trying to take it all in. This was one of those simple tests that just told you whether you were pregnant or not, so in a cloud of excitement we drove up to the big Tesco and got a Clearblue one that tells you how many weeks gone you are. I don't remember feeling any embarrassment this time – there were so many other things to think about!

'Five to six weeks!' I said.

This time I watched the test like a hawk as I waited for the result to appear. I looked at Ashley and he was absolutely buzzing. My mind was racing as I tried to work out the dates. The baby would be due in August 2020, the same month as my birthday – 'A little Leo,' I said. 'Same as me.'

We went back out to the supermarket, because Ashley wanted to buy some alcohol to celebrate and I fancied some strawberry Yazoos. I'd been drinking them like they were going out of fashion. I should have realised something was going on, because I've never been into strawberry milkshakes before, but suddenly I was craving them so badly.

Ashley partied all night long in the apartment we lived in at the time, dancing and drinking for hours and hours. I joined in for as long as I could, sipping my milkshake and marvelling at how this had happened and how our lives were going to change. It was the most amazing night, a huge celebration of the brand-new life we had created together.

. . .

'I love you,' I heard Ashley say.

I turned my head to look at him. He was looking straight past me, talking to Azaylia in her cot beside me. 'You're so precious,' he went on. 'You're amazing, do you know that? You're *incredible*!'

These were all things he used to say to Azaylia when she was a bump. 'I love you, you're so precious' – I'd heard that every day, countless times a day, month after month throughout my pregnancy. 'I can't wait to meet you,' he always added.

We both smiled, thinking the same thought as we lay side by side. The wait was over, we'd met her at last. Our daughter was here, in all her amazing glory.

Right at the start, when I found out I was expecting, Ashley had wanted a boy. There are lots of strong males on his dad's side of the family and he's still a lad's lad at heart, so I guess his gut reaction was inevitable.

'Matty,' he said, sharing the news I was pregnant with one of his two brothers. 'You're gonna be an uncle again!'

'You know what, brother, so are you!' came the reply.

'No way!'

The siblings immediately started talking about the fact they would both have boys. 'Course we'll have boys!' they said. 'Gotta both be boys!'

For a while I thought I'd like a boy too, though for very different reasons. I'd been through a lot of pain in my life and I didn't want my child to suffer like I had. It shocks me to remember how I felt. I thought a boy would face fewer difficulties in life, purely because of his gender. I know that's a generalisation, but that's what I thought. Witnessing the breakdown of my parents' marriage had scarred me. Mum was the one who suffered. She was left to bring the kids up on her own, juggling two jobs, while my dad gradually drifted off the scene. And then it was me, stuck in a bad relationship. I was the female and I was the one who was suffering. I should have got out of the relationship sooner than I did, but I was not the strong, proud woman I am today. Life had been sapped out of me so skilfully I didn't even see it happening.

How different life was when I settled down with Ashley.

When I was sixteen weeks pregnant, we'd paid for a private scan to find out our baby's gender. Waiting until the birth was not an option I entertained for one second. I'm a planner, I was stuck in lockdown and had a nursery to decorate and a wardrobe to fill! I wanted to know the sex as soon as I possibly could and Ashley was in agreement.

The previous two scans we'd had – at eight and twelve weeks – had been joyful experiences. We were blown away by the images we saw on the screen. It was so affirming, seeing everything was as it should be, and we were buzzing for days afterwards. I loved all the positive energy we took from the scans – it was exactly what I wanted to wrap myself in during my pregnancy.

Ever since I was a little girl I'd had a feeling that you could talk to the universe, in a way. I'd think of a song and it would come on the radio, or I'd deliberately block out negative thoughts to stop bad things coming true. It didn't always work, of course, but I still stuck to my belief and way of behaving. Why wouldn't I, if some good might come from it?

As an adult, reading *The Secret* by Rhonda Byrne really reso-nated with me. Her beliefs about the law of attraction and the idea that a person's thoughts have the potential to change the course of their life really spoke to me. She had basically given a name and an explanation to what I'd been doing, or trying to do, all my life. After that, I became even more convinced by the law of attraction, which meant that, when I was pregnant, I made sure I thought positive thoughts every single day. Everything was going to be OK, I told myself. Any negative thoughts that crept in were swiftly banished, because they would only make me poorly and drain me emotionally, and that was not healthy for the baby.

On the way to the scan, we got diverted. 'Oh look, the road's closed,' I said to Ashley. 'We'll have to follow the signs.' We found ourselves travelling down a road we'd never been on before, going round the houses to get to the clinic. Out of nowhere, a pink balloon appeared, flying up in front of the car.

'Ashley, pink balloon!' I shouted. 'That's a sign!'

He laughed, which is often his reaction when I come out with stuff like that, though he had to admit this was a very timely coincidence. 'What if we come out and it's a girl?' I said. 'It has to be a girl! It's a pink balloon, it's a sign!'

'Well, let's go and see, Safiyya,' Ashley told me. 'Let's see what the universe has in store for us.'

We'd agreed that we didn't want the sonographer to reveal the baby's gender during the scan. Our plan was to get her to write it down, then we'd take the scan away with us and do the gender reveal at home with close family around us. We had it all planned – we'd pop a balloon and the gender would be written down inside, so we'd all find out at the same time. Then, once all our loved ones had been told, we'd share the news on social media. Our Instagram followers had been so supportive when we told them we were having a baby and we'd been overwhelmed by all their messages: 'You two are going to be the best parents,' they posted. 'Congratulations!', 'You're going to have a beautiful baby, you're such a cute couple', 'Amazing, you're going to be the best mummy.'

We also got some cheeky messages along the lines of, 'You're going to grow up, finally it's time!' but the response was overwhelmingly positive. We didn't expect such a massive reaction. It was incredible and the support encouraged both of us to keep sharing our baby journey online.

I had no idea what I was looking at when the baby scan started to shimmer onto the monitor next to me, but Ashley obviously had a better eye than me.

'It's not got a winky,' he blurted out.

I shot him a look as if to say, 'How do you know? You don't know how to read a scan!' and then I made the mistake of looking at the sonographer. She was also giving Ashley a look, one that said, 'He's got it!' After that we didn't do the big gender reveal the way we had planned it – we just told the family our news instead.

Despite seeing the pink balloon in the road, I was really surprised we were having a girl. I'd started to totally believe we were having a boy, what with Ashley's initial response and the worries I had about having a girl. There was also the fact that my brother had a boy, which somehow made me think I'd be more likely to have one – all the signs had seemed to be suggesting that was our destiny.

Ashley was overjoyed. We were having a little princess, that's how he saw it, right from that moment. When the news sank in, I was so happy too and I felt so blessed. I'd had so many insecurities about having a girl, but now I started to wonder if maybe that was why I was given one.

Perhaps I *needed* to have a little girl, to help me learn and grow.

CHAPTER
FOUR

'Look at us!' I laughed. 'Changing nappies instead of partying!'
Matty's girlfriend, Amy, had her baby girl six days before I
had Azaylia. It was meant to be the other way round, but Anaya
came early and then of course Azaylia went over her due date,
finally arriving on 10 August 2020. The Covid restrictions had
eased and this was the first time we'd all managed to get together
for a proper family celebration to welcome the two little princesses. I was breastfeeding so I wasn't drinking, but I wasn't
interested in alcohol or staying up late: I was being a mum and
making sure my little girl had everything she needed. This was
my dream and I was in my element, loving every moment. Ashley
was so happy too. This was the life we had both dreamed of.

After we'd changed the babies' bums, Amy and I stayed
upstairs in the bedroom, away from the music and noise, feeding
our little girls and giggling about how wrong Ashley and Matty
had been about having boys.

'Who'd have thought it?' I said. 'Two beautiful baby girls. We're going to have so much fun, watching them grow together.'

Azaylia was dressed in a pink Moschino sleepsuit with a bear on the front and she had a little Gucci coat to travel in. The coat was a crazy thing to buy, really, because she'd grow out of it in five minutes, but I couldn't resist it. My mum bought her little Dior coats too and she had some beautiful Versace sleepsuits. I made sure Azaylia's outfits always had matching headbands and pretty socks, and whatever I bought, I always felt the material to make sure it was soft enough and wouldn't chafe or scratch her skin.

In the beginning, Ashley glazed over a bit when I showed him the baby clothes online that I wanted to buy, but then he spotted some Nike twinsets to match his own. He bought those as well as some Nike vests and even a pair of Jordans shoes, which made me laugh.

'It'll be a while before she can train with you,' I said.

'But she will,' he insisted, 'she will.'

Ashley had decided he'd like our daughter to be a professional tennis player when she grew up.

'Why?' I asked, thinking football would have been a more obvious choice.

'Look at her hands! She's got strong hands. It's a very cool sport, she'll be amazing at it.'

It warmed my heart to hear Ashley dreaming of the future. As for me, I didn't have an opinion on what job she might do. All I knew was that I wanted her to be stylish, well-mannered and grounded, and successful in everything she wanted to achieve for herself. Ashley approved of that completely.

By now I was posting lots of pictures of Azaylia on Instagram. I did it because I was so proud to show her off, and I didn't expect anything in return. At the time I only had about 4,000 followers but I'd get hundreds, if not thousands of lovely responses. The love and support astonished me and spurred me on to keep sharing the joy.

One day I posted a picture of Azaylia in her car seat. I didn't know whether I was meant to take her coat off before I strapped her in so I asked the question on Instagram, hoping someone out there might have the same seat and be able to give me advice. I immediately received stacks of helpful replies, with people also making sure I knew how to tilt the seat and make all sorts of adjustments. It was brilliant – like having a back-up army of support – and all from people I didn't even know. If there were people out there who thought I was over-sharing, I didn't look for it and I didn't care. When Azaylia was grown up, I wanted her to be able to look back and see how proud I was of her, and how wanted she was, and loved and cared for. That was my priority. I wanted her to have the security and stability that I didn't always have and to see that every last detail was thought about, and that she was cherished and never went without a thing.

I was finally moving around without pains shooting through my body and at last I was enjoying motherhood in the way I'd imagined it would be. The sun was shining the first time I took Azaylia out in her pram. I'd pictured this moment for so long.

Ever since we decided to try for a baby I imagined pushing a pram, showing off my baby to everyone around me, and at last it was becoming a reality.

'Let's go, princess!' I said.

Azaylia was bright-eyed and looked a million dollars lying in her new pram. All I did was walk down the road into town, but it was one of the best trips of my life. Every neighbour who saw me and anyone and everyone I said hello to in town broke into a big, beaming smile as they peeped in the pram, said congratulations and told me how beautiful my daughter was. I felt like I was floating across the pavements.

Ashley continued being a very hands-on dad, even though I was fully back on my feet. I couldn't fault him and we were having so much fun. We took Azaylia to Drayton Manor theme park when she was just four weeks old, along with some members of the family.

'Daddy's still got to have some fun too!' Ashley wrote on Instagram, under a photo of him cradling Azaylia in his arms. I loved the picture. Drayton Manor was a place Ashley and I had been to together before. I looked up an old photo of us on a ride, screaming and having a laugh. It was taken only three years before, but we looked like kids. We had no responsibilities at all and we were having a ball. I'd gone from feeling miserable to plodding along and then – pow! – my life had exploded with happiness. Every day I'd wake up and feel excited to be with Ashley, wondering what we were doing next and where we'd be going.

I kept scrolling, smiling at some of my favourite memories. There we were on holiday in Turkey. Ashley was having his teeth done – a full set of crowns to give him a 'smile makeover' – and I went with him. We didn't ever want to be apart and we had a blast, jet-skiing, posing on the beach and going out to bars and clubs. We were in our own world together, running around and making so many happy memories. Me and Ashley had love, we had friendship, we had excitement. We were having adventures together, we were best friends and we were lovers. It was amazing – we really did have it all.

On Valentine's Day he took me out for dinner in Leicester and when we arrived at the restaurant there were red roses and balloons on the table and champagne on ice. Everyone in the room looked over, as if to say, 'oh my God, that's amazing! That's for you! That's so beautiful!' I'd never had that before. Ashley took a photo of me, smiling. He was proud to post it up and it was so refreshing to be with someone who wanted to make me feel good and show me off. He always made me feel special, whether we were on a trip to the zoo, having a snowball fight in the street or on a glitzy night out at a TV awards ceremony. Even if we just had a Costa together he'd want to take my picture. 'Oh no!' I'd say if I didn't feel I looked right, but Ashley wouldn't have it – 'Come on, you look beautiful!' In my old life, I'd been verbally abused for posting up a picture with a friend, drinking a glass of wine. That was one of the many things that stripped me of my confidence and self-esteem, but Ashley was helping rebuild me. Every day it felt like he was pulling the old me back out of myself, reminding me who I was and who I should be.

All our pictures warmed my heart. 'Complete', 'soul mates', 'best friends', 'couple goals' – these were my hashtags I used under the photos of us together. After a weekend break to Center Parcs with all his family, I wrote, 'I'm the reason behind your smile and you're the reason I'm so happy'.

I looked at him now. Our feelings hadn't changed, but everything was so different. We were still having fun and enjoying every moment together, but our focus was on Azaylia and making sure she had everything she needed.

It was September now and there was a chill in the air. I'd dressed Azaylia in a white snowsuit for Drayton Manor and she was very cosy and contented, but even so, I was checking her all the time. Do you think she might be too hot? Does she need feeding? What about her nappy?

Me and Ashley were both on it, all the time. Parenthood was our new adventure and we were lapping it up and learning fast. We were both proper adults now. That's how it felt, and we wouldn't change a single thing.

· · ·

After being such a contented baby for the first few weeks, Azaylia started to become restless.

'I think she wants bouncing,' I said to Ashley.

Azaylia was grumbling and crying but, sure enough, as soon as Ashley bounced her gently in his arms, walking round and round the living room, she settled down. 'She needs bouncing' became a very well-used phrase in our house, but then Azaylia's crying went up a gear and no amount of bouncing would settle her. She seemed to be not just unsettled, but distressed, and she was crying non-stop, showing no signs of letting up.

'What do we do?' Ashley said.

I'd tried bouncing her, cradling her and swaddling her, but nothing worked. We were scratching our heads and starting to really worry. Azaylia had been fed and burped and she was clean and changed. We'd bathed her and tried laying her in various different positions to get her comfortable, but she still wouldn't stop crying.

'I'm going to call the clinic,' I said. 'This isn't right. It's probably something simple we're missing.'

There were plenty of experienced mothers in the family I could have turned to, but I wanted a professional opinion. I'd trained as a dental nurse when I was in my early twenties, which was my route into becoming an aesthetic practitioner. My experience had made me a firm believer in dealing with experts who have studied for years and I wouldn't want to put my loved ones on the spot.

You could only have a face-to-face appointment if it was an emergency and so I settled for a telephone consultation. The duty doctor listened to my concerns and suggested that I might not be producing enough milk – 'Try topping her up with some formula,' was the advice. 'She could be hungry.'

Azaylia had been gaining weight. I'd had a midwife call at the house and she'd weighed Azaylia, so it had never occurred to me that she wasn't getting enough milk. But I went straight out to the big Tesco to buy some top-up bottles of Aptamil formula milk, as the doctor suggested. Azaylia guzzled them and was much more settled than she had been for days. I felt a pang of guilt: how could I have let my baby go hungry?

'Well done, Azaylia,' I told her. 'I'm sorry Mummy didn't give you enough milk, but it won't happen again, I promise! Me and Daddy are learning every day and we are here to take care of you.'

• • •

I went out to work for the first time when Azaylia was almost six weeks old. It was always my intention to be a working mum. For one thing, I didn't ever want to rely on Ashley financially and if I bought him a present I wanted to be able to buy it with money I'd earned myself but, most importantly, I wanted to be a role model for Azaylia. When she was older, I wanted her to watch her mummy go out to work and see a grounded, strong and independent woman, one with a strong work ethic. My plan was to take on clients in the aesthetic beauty clinic two days a week, when either Ashley or one of our mums could look after Azaylia.

Ashley was in charge today and that made it as easy as possible for me.

'Bye bye, princess,' I said, kissing Azaylia's cheek. 'You be a good girl for Daddy, yeah?'

She gurgled contentedly. Ever since she'd been having top-up milk, Azaylia had been less unsettled, though she was still crying on and off. Seeing her in Ashley's arms, being bounced and loved, gave me the courage I needed to walk out of the front door and go back to work. I'd expressed some breast milk and left everything in its place to hopefully make Ashley's day with Azaylia run as smoothly as it possibly could.

Me and my brother spoke on the phone every day and he called me that afternoon.

'How's it going?' Danny asked. 'You OK?'

'I'm so excited to finish work!' I said. 'Normally I'm thinking about getting in, putting my feet up and chilling, but all I can think is, how long till I get to see her?'

He laughed, knowing the feeling so well. 'I'm really happy for you,' he said.

Ashley had everything under control at home. He rang to say he was having a ball with Azaylia and that they were chilling and listening to music together. His mum had been round to give him some support, he said, which was lovely.

When I got home, Ashley was giving Azaylia a bottle and the two of them were snuggled up on the sofa. Azaylia was drinking the milk greedily, I was pleased to see. 'What a little champ!' I said, looking around the room. There was baby paraphernalia everywhere. Mrs Hinch would have had a fit, but this was my new life and I *loved* it.

That same week, I returned to the gym for the first time, just for a very light workout. My head told me this was a healthy thing to do. It would do me good to have some 'me' time and it was right that Ashley and Azaylia had time together to bond as father and daughter.

I quite enjoyed my workout, but at the same time I was so excited to walk out of the gym and head back to my baby. I felt that mummy magnet pulling me home. Azaylia was just six weeks old and there was a voice in the back of my head asking, 'what am I going to walk into?' When I stepped through the door I felt the most powerful rush of love. Everything was very quiet and there on the rug, lying side by side, were Ashley and Azaylia, both sleeping contentedly. I stood rooted to the spot, drinking in the beautiful scene. Motherhood was more magical than I could ever have imagined. In my perfect baby daughter I'd found everything I didn't even know was missing from my life. *How did I ever live without you, Azaylia?* I thought.

By now we'd had a few more telephone consultations with the doctor. Azaylia didn't have her routine six-week injection because she was bunged up on the day and we were advised to wait until she was feeling better. She loved the bottled milk, but we noticed she had a bit of a hard, bloated tummy and her breathing sounded very snuffly and congested. She also had gunk building up in her eyes and she was still crying quite a lot.

'If you're worried, call the doctor,' Ashley said, every time without fail. 'Don't hesitate.'

In one phone consultation I was told that she probably had colic and she should take something called Infacol, which I could buy over the counter at the chemist. I'd never even heard of colic, but the diagnosis seemed to make sense. Colic can cause crying in healthy babies for no apparent reason, I discovered, or it could be that they are having trouble digesting their food. Maybe

Azaylia was just adjusting to the formula milk? We hoped that giving drops of Infacol on the tongue could help with wind and any griping pain, so I bought several bottles and gave her the maximum dose every day.

The colicky crying was still coming and going, but even so Azaylia was an easy, undemanding baby. I didn't identify with mums who went on about the endless hard work and sleepless nights. The crying only bothered me because I was worried I was still missing something I could be doing to help my daughter be more settled.

When I told the doctor about the congested breathing and the gunky eyes, we were given a nasal spray and told to keep an eye on her. The spray didn't seem to do any good and then Azaylia had trouble filling her nappy. She was prescribed laxatives to put in her milk for that.

Blimey, I thought, looking at the stash of medication on her shelf. *I had no idea newborn babies could have all these ailments.*

Then one day I noticed she had spots of blood in her nappy. I stayed calm and called the GP, telling myself not to panic. As a new mum, I was on a steep learning curve and this was probably nothing to worry about. Sure enough, I was told to just keep monitoring it and let them know if it happened again. It did, and this time I photographed the nappy and emailed the image over to the surgery. 'Just keep monitoring,' they said, which I was so relieved about.

When I'd taken Azaylia for her six-week injection, I took a lot of comfort from seeing a doctor in person. The clinic had her full medical history on file and now a doctor had seen her in the flesh, which was so reassuring. I'd reported everything – the snuffling that made it sound like she was struggling to breathe, the fact she was crying a lot, the hard tummy, the constipation. Azaylia was also not drinking the quantity of milk she should have been and I told the GP I was worried about that too. The advice was still to keep doing what we were doing and to let the doctor know if anything else happened, or we had any other concerns.

I was grateful that the GP didn't seem worried, but a professional opinion didn't make it any easier to watch Azaylia struggle with all these different problems. The colic made her writhe around, her tummy so tight and her little face all red and scrunched up. Whenever she was unsettled, Ashley bounced her in his arms. He danced with her and we both sang to her. We also gave her lots of warm baths and cuddles, but nothing seemed to soothe her. That's the problem with colic, I was hearing. As tough as it was to see our daughter like that, we just had to wait for it to pass and for Azaylia to eventually grow out of it.

. . .

'Who's a beautiful girl?' I said, lifting Azaylia from her cot. She was in a very contented mood and she looked straight into my eyes. It was a lovely moment, one that made me feel incredibly close and connected to my daughter.

'Shall I let you into a secret?'

Ashley's thirtieth birthday was coming up, at the end of September 2020, and I really wanted to spoil him and make it a special day for him. I'd bought him a really good massage gun because he gets knots all over his body from training so hard and my thumbs were always aching like mad from trying to smooth them out.

'Mummy's thumbs won't snap off now!' I said to Azaylia, telling her all about the present. 'Won't Daddy be pleased!'

Azaylia was in such a lovely, peaceful mood and she was gurgling away as I carried on talking to her. I loved our little chats. Ashley was in the shower and this was our girly gossip time. I told her all about the family party I'd organised and the fabulous birthday cake I'd ordered.

'Hey, baby! Aren't we going to have a lovely time?' I said as I carried her downstairs.

Under the kitchen spotlights I noticed Azaylia had some white spots on her tongue: 'Oh my goodness, what's going on now? I think we better check this out.'

I didn't think twice about calling the GP again. I have so much respect and faith in the medical profession and it was always very easy to get through. No matter how minor the problem, they never once made me feel like a nervy, panicking mother.

'It's thrush,' the GP told me straight away. 'Nothing to worry about, it's very common in babies.'

'I had no idea babies could get thrush,' I said.

The doctor reassured me that thrush is not serious and would probably go away on its own in a few days. I was to call again if it didn't.

We had a wonderful time celebrating Ashley's birthday. I invited all the family over to party and he was absolutely blown away by the cake I'd had made for the occasion. It had pictures from all the big moments in his life – playing football, appearing on *Take Me Out* and *The Challenge*, working for MTV, DJing, the lot. The pictures were presented like clips on an old-style film reel that curled around the cake.

'Our journey together has been so beautiful, fun and amazing,' I wrote on my Instagram, under a photo of us all glammed up and ready to party. 'It just gets better and better.'

CHAPTER FIVE

A reminder popped up on my phone. 'MANCHESTER' it said, in scary-looking capital letters. '9th October 2020'. My heart raced a little bit. This was going to be a big day for Ashley and me. We each had some work in Manchester – I was doing some training in a clinic and he had some filming to do for his fitness and personal training app, Beast Fit. But it wasn't the work that fazed me. This would be the very first time we were both leaving Azaylia. Manchester was only two hours away, we'd be there and back in a day and we were leaving Azaylia with my mum. Even so, it felt like a very big deal.

In the days leading up to the trip I was in full-on planning mode, sorting out exactly what I needed to pack for Azaylia. As any new mum knows, eight-week-old babies don't travel light and I felt like I was organising a two-week holiday. Meanwhile, I hadn't given a second thought to what I was going to wear or how I was going to present myself that day – that was the very last thing on my mind.

The thrush on Azaylia's tongue didn't shift by itself and so she'd had to have some medicine for that. She still had the Infacol, the nasal spray and the laxatives too, yet her colicky symptoms, snuffly breathing and the straining to fill her nappy had not gone away.

The day before our trip I was making a note of all the instructions I'd need to give to my mum when I left Azaylia with her. *Colic, congestion, constipation, thrush … what a shame my baby girl had to put up with all that*, I thought.

Azaylia needed her nappy changing and so I laid her on the changing mat and took off her sleepsuit. I thought how pretty she looked, lying there in just her nappy. Her bright blue eyes were shining out of her face and I wanted to capture the moment, which wasn't unusual. I was taking pictures of Azaylia every day and she seemed to love the camera, always staring straight at it and gurgling away.

'Don't you look beautiful!' I said, holding up my phone.

Oh, what's that?

I did a double take, because through the lens of my iPhone the skin on Azaylia's tummy looked mottled. I put the phone down and examined her, but when I looked with my naked eye, the mottling was barely visible. *Strange*, I thought. I looked again through the camera lens and once again the mottling was much more noticeable. I took a picture, deciding I should email it to the doctor, just to be on the safe side.

I wondered if Azaylia was cold, so I started getting her changed and dressed as quickly as possible. As soon as I opened up her nappy I spotted a little bruise near the bottom of her tummy. I instinctively ran my finger across it, because I knew from my nursing training that a bruise should be flat on the skin, with no hardness underneath. It should also disappear when you push down on it and reappear when you let go. I felt a little bit of a lump underneath the bruise, which was worrying. I couldn't imagine how Azaylia had managed to get a little bash there, or how I hadn't noticed it last time I changed her nappy, which was only a couple of hours earlier. But I didn't panic: as with everything else, there was bound to be a simple explanation, I told myself.

'Can you have a look at this?' I wrote in an email to the GP, explaining how the mottling and bruise had just appeared, seemingly from nowhere. The surgery had closed for the evening, so the next morning I called to let them know I'd sent the email. The receptionist told me she'd received the picture and would get a doctor to look at it ASAP.

I started having second thoughts about leaving Azaylia with my mum.

'Shall we take her with us?' I said to Ashley.

We quickly decided it wasn't the right thing to do. She was colicky and we thought she'd be much better off with my mum, rather than strapped in a car seat for hours. Mum was really looking forward to having her and of course she was perfectly capable of taking care of her granddaughter, even if she was a bit niggly.

When we dropped Azaylia off, I ran through all of her medications and double-checked I'd given Mum every piece of clothing and equipment she could possibly need.

'You two go and enjoy a bit of time together,' Mum smiled. 'Go on, I can look after her, don't you worry!'

I gave Azaylia a big kiss and told her I'd miss her: 'Be a good girl! See you later!'

'We love you, baby!' Ashley said, also planting a big kiss on her cheek.

I adored the way he always gazed at Azaylia, a look of total adoration filling his face.

And so I drove to Manchester. In the very short window between the end of lockdown and Azaylia being born, I'd quickly swapped my little white two-seater Audi TT for a four-door grey Mercedes. I love cars but I literally bought the first one I looked at because I was so worried about having something big enough to fix the car seat into. It was safe and it was comfortable, that's what mattered now. Our lives had changed in such a short space of time: Azaylia's safety and comfort came first, second and third.

The drive to Manchester brought mixed emotions. Mum had done a very good job of reassuring me Azaylia would be absolutely fine without us. I was enjoying the freedom of driving up the motorway like I used to before Azaylia was born and it was great to put on some music and spend some uninterrupted time with Ashley. But that mummy magnet was still so powerful. I was learning that you don't have time with or without your child. Mother and child have an unbreakable bond, and that means you have time away from your baby, but she is always with you, in your heart and mind, no matter how far apart you are.

My phone rang seconds after we pulled up in Manchester.

'Great!' I said. 'It's the surgery.'

I answered the call eagerly, fully expecting to be told not to worry about the mottling or the bruise. It was all perfectly fine …

'You need to take your daughter to A&E straight away.'

My heart dropped to my stomach.

'What?'

I was so shocked. 'Why? What's wrong with her?' I could hardly get the words out, it was as if an icy hand had grabbed my throat.

It was a duty GP who had looked at the photographs. He was calm and polite, repeating that Azaylia needed to be checked over, straight away, in hospital.

'Can you get her to A&E right away?'

'Why? What is it?'

Ashley was looking at me in alarm, asking what was going on.

'That's what we need to find out.'

The words were banging round my head and I was starting to shake. All at once I was talking to Ashley and trying to explain to the GP that I was two hours away and that Azaylia wasn't even with me.

'Who is looking after her? I see. Then you need to get your mother to take her to A&E. Can she do that straight away?'

Mum picked up my call immediately. 'Mum, you need to take Azaylia to A&E,' I blurted. 'I've just had a call …'

'I'm already in an ambulance,' she replied, 'so don't worry.'

'What? How?'

I was so bewildered, especially as Mum sounded so calm.

'Don't worry,' she repeated. 'Relax. Azaylia's with me and I'm just going to get her checked over.'

She told me they were on their way to Walsgrave Hospital in Coventry. They had clearly started their journey before I'd had the call from my GP, so what on earth was going on? Me and Ashley looked at each other in confusion and disbelief. The situation felt so surreal and nothing was making sense.

I could hear Mum saying that she had called 111 and they sent for an ambulance. It sounded like my head was plunged deep in a bucket and she was talking to me through water. 'I didn't want to worry you while you were away,' I heard her say. 'But she didn't seem right. She was very congested and I thought it would be good to get some medical advice.'

I was finally starting to put two and two together. It was purely coincidental that Mum had headed off in an ambulance at exactly the same time as the GP was calling me but why was this suddenly such an emergency?

'We'll come straight to the hospital,' I said. 'We're on our way. Tell Azaylia we love her very much. Give her big kisses from Mummy and Daddy. Ring when you get there, please.'

We turned the car around and headed straight back to the motorway, both of us stunned into silence. There was a riot going on inside my body. Fear had cascaded in and sparks of panic were pulsing through my nerves. I started forcing positive thoughts into my head, desperately trying to keep things in perspective.

Azaylia is going to be absolutely fine. We saw her two hours ago. Mum was being cautious and that's why she was so calm. She could have waited until we got back from Manchester, but then Mum's not like that. If she thinks something needs doing, she takes control and gets the job done. Look, we have an unwritten rule in the family that we don't pass on bad news to anyone when we're apart. We wait until we're back together. That's what we did if someone broke their arm on holiday. What's the point of sharing that and worrying everyone?

But it wasn't working and my panic was rising.

This is not a broken arm! It's Azaylia, my precious baby girl! It doesn't matter what Mum did. The GP was sending Azaylia to A&E in any case! He saw those pictures and immediately wanted her admitted. What on earth is wrong with my baby?

When we stopped at traffic lights I stole a sideways glance at Ashley. He was very still and silent, his eyes focused firmly on the road in front and his lips set in a steely grimace. He flicked me a glance and tried to speak. 'Safiyya ...' he started, but he had no words. What was there to say? We were in the dark right now and it was a terrifying place to be.

I started sobbing. I told myself I had to keep it together for Azaylia, but I was struggling to breathe normally, let alone stop crying. We drove on in silence and I started thinking about the bruise on Azaylia's tummy. One little bruise could be explained, I'd thought. Maybe she'd bashed herself with a toy, or maybe I'd caused it somehow, when I was changing her nappy in the night and was half asleep, or as I lifted her out of the bath. They were the explanations I'd turned over in my mind. Simple, innocent explanations. I hadn't been overly worried, that's all I was expecting to hear from the GP. Maybe I'd be given a routine appointment to go into the surgery with Azaylia, or to see my midwife the following week, just for a check-up, in case she needed some other medicine.

My phone rang again, sending more shockwaves through my body. Mum was on loudspeaker so we could both hear, but my head was in that bucket of water again, the words distorted as they bubbled into my brain.

'Her white blood cell count is very high.'

Mum still sounded in control but there was an anxious edge to her voice now. The tears were splashing down my face and I couldn't stop crying long enough to get two words out.

'What does that mean?' It was Ashley who was speaking now. 'What's normal? What's it meant to be?'

Mum said Azaylia's count was above fifty, which was extremely high for an adult, let alone an eight-week-old baby. All the words were washing over each other and I couldn't take anything in. I just wanted to get to my baby and see for myself what was going on. I didn't understand anything about white blood cell counts or what they meant.

'Ashley, what's wrong with her?' I was sobbing uncontrollably.

'Safiyya, try to calm down,' Ashley soothed, but his voice was shaking.

Neither of us spoke again for a while. From time to time we gave each other a look of reassurance or disbelief, or both. There were 50mph traffic restrictions all along our route back and I wanted to rip through them all. We couldn't get to the hospital fast enough, but we had to be patient. It was like a slow torture.

By the time we arrived at University Hospitals Coventry and Warwickshire we'd spoken to Mum a third time. Azaylia's white blood cell count was 200. It was such a big number.

'Two hundred?' I could hear the fear in Ashley's voice as his words ricocheted around my skull. He was asking where we had to go, which ward she was on. It was like he was on autopilot, keeping everything going, trying to stay calm when his head was exploding just like mine.

We ran across the car park. I'd never felt so much comfort from having Ashley by my side; without him I'm not sure I'd have been able to put one foot in front of the other. To reach Azaylia we had to go through two white screens that were zipped up. I'd never seen a set-up like this before. When I unzipped the second screen and stepped through it, I saw a sea of doctors and nurses. Azaylia was in a plastic cot that looked exactly like the one she'd slept in as a newborn. My heart went out to her and I wanted to scoop her into my arms and carry her out of there, back to normality. She looked just as beautiful as she did on the day she was born, but now she had wires attached to her body and was wriggling and crying as a nurse stuck a needle into her little hand. The medics let me through.

'Mummy and Daddy are here,' I said, peering into the cot and stroking her head.

The nurse needed to take some blood from Azaylia, but they couldn't find a vein. I took hold of Azaylia's other hand and stroked her hair softly: 'Be brave,' I told her.

I understood that her temperature had been spiking and they needed to control that too, but I didn't ask how or why. My instincts told me to focus on comforting Azaylia as best I could. Answers and explanations could wait. As soon as the doctors and nurses had done their work, we'd get all the answers we were searching for. We'd know exactly what was wrong with Azaylia and she would have all the treatment she needed.

I have no idea what Ashley was doing at this point, or my mum or anybody else. It was as if I was looking down a tunnel and all I could see was Azaylia at the end of it. The nurses were repeatedly tapping Azaylia's little hands and I didn't like it. I knew they were only doing their best to get into her veins, but it was hard to watch.

'It's alright. You're going to be alright, baby.'

I put my arm up over Azaylia's face so she couldn't see what was going on.

• • •

'Please, come and take a seat.'

We were still in the emergency room at University Hospitals Coventry and Warwickshire. Another doctor appeared and he was indicating to me and Ashley to sit down. His expression was stern and serious, and that terrified me. This was not going to be good news and I could already feel the earth shift beneath my feet. I found myself catching my breath, waiting to see what would fall down around me.

'What's wrong with our daughter?'

The doctor took a breath and spoke kindly but very directly.

'Azaylia has leukaemia,' she said.

Leukaemia?

I didn't know what leukaemia was, so it was actually the next sentence that shot through my ears like daggers.

'And she needs to go to Birmingham Children's Hospital immediately.'

Whatever this leukaemia was, Azaylia's condition was obviously very serious. There was no time to waste and we had to go right now, as quickly as possible.

I went into emergency mode instantly, which was something I was used to doing at work. If a patient fainted in a dental surgery or a clinic I didn't go to pieces and panic. I was trained to keep my professional head on, deal with the situation as swiftly as possible and only react emotionally once the patient was back on their feet. That's what I was instinctively doing now. I was in tears and I was terrified, but it was all systems go to get Azaylia to Birmingham. Things were happening at a hundred miles an hour, but that was a good thing. It was a 25-mile journey and the sooner we got there, the sooner Azaylia would be given the medicine or surgery she needed to make her better.

Me and Ashley followed the ambulance in my car. My mind was focused sharply on the emergency situation we were in and I was thinking about practicalities. The Covid rules meant I couldn't leave my car in the hospital car park in Coventry and in any case we'd need it for when we took Azaylia home from Birmingham.

At the same time my head was exploding with anxiety.

I can't believe this is happening, I can't believe what's going on. How are we in this situation?

All of these panic-stricken thoughts were swirling round my head but I didn't let any of them escape onto my lips and I didn't collapse. Ashley was the same – we had both clicked into survival mode without even thinking about it.

Birmingham is one of the best children's hospitals in the country, I told him. We were very lucky it was so close to where we lived and Azaylia would get the best treatment in the world for whatever this illness was. That's what we had to focus on. It clearly wasn't going to be an easy ride: this was a serious situation and she was a very poorly little girl right now but we'd be with her every step of the way, helping her through this as quickly as possible. Then we could all go back home, where we belonged, together.

CHAPTER SIX

I curled up in a ball next to Ashley's feet at the bottom of the pull-out chair bed. It was very late now and he was asleep, at last. I told him to take the bed. He was absolutely exhausted, wiped out; we both were. I'd sat for hours in the plastic chair next to Azaylia's hospital cot, watching her breathe. There were tabs connected to her body and wires everywhere. I had no idea what anything was for. Her little face had puffed up so much, her eyes were like slits. I was relieved she was asleep now too, because seeing her struggle to open her eyes had been heart-wrenching.

The swelling in Azaylia's face had already started when we were in Coventry. Her body wasn't dealing with fluid properly, that's what we'd been told. I didn't know any more than that and I still had no idea what leukaemia was.

All the nurses were brilliant, monitoring Azaylia and attending to her constantly. She looked peaceful and comfortable as she slept, which was a blessing. I took it as a sign that she was already getting better, now she was in hospital and getting all the care she needed.

'How long will you need to keep her in?' I asked.

The nurse looked unsure, or was it not her place to tell me?

'The consultant will come and talk to you,' she said softly.

I didn't Google anything and I didn't even ask Ashley what he knew about leukaemia, or if he'd even heard of it – I wanted to hear it from the experts.

Ashley had been very quiet and when I looked at him he was like a blank canvas, any expression in his face ironed flat by shock and disbelief. We barely spoke a word to each other, but I could feel his presence all the time. We were in this together, we were a family and he was there for us – that's all I needed to know. The spotlight was on Azaylia. Everything was about Azaylia. We were just shadowy satellites floating in her orbit.

I was wearing a bodysuit, skirt, tights and boots, all in black. It was an outfit I'd hastily put together for Manchester, once all of Azaylia's packing for the day was done. I had a long black jacket too, which had become a blanket for my legs as I curled up in the plastic chair. I'd lost track of time. Our trip to Manchester felt like a week ago, not a journey we'd made earlier the same day.

You have to close your eyes, I told myself, *even if only to rest them*.

As soon as I shut my eyes I heard Azaylia murmur. I shot to my feet straight away and my caesarean scar reminded me – angrily – that it was still there, as did the milk in my swollen breasts. I hadn't given either a single thought until now.

'Azaylia,' I whispered, 'Mummy's here, baby. It's alright. How are you feeling?'

But she wasn't waking up. She must have just murmured in her sleep, but perhaps there was a chance she might hear me? I keep talking to her, just in case.

'Daddy's here too. We're both here for you. We love you so much. Get well soon, baby.'

. . .

A nurse came in to tell me they were going to insert a central line. We'd been in overnight by now, and it was Saturday afternoon.

'What's that?' I asked. I'd never heard of one before.

The nurse explained that Azaylia's medicine would go in through this tube, which was bigger than a normal IV line and it would go directly through her chest and into a vein. It could also be used to deliver fluids, blood or to give her nutrients if she needed them, as well as to draw blood. I wasn't taking it in, or allowing myself to dwell on why she needed all this. Ashley looked so worried and scared, and he was saying very little.

When Azaylia was born, I'd marvelled at how perfect her little hands were. I'd counted her fingers and thumbs and couldn't believe how flawless her skin was. I didn't want her to have needles stuck into her hands again, ever. The memory of her little hand being tapped and tapped as the nurse struggled to find a vein had played on my mind. At least that wouldn't have to happen again, once she had this central line in.

I didn't ask what medicine would be going in through this central line. I didn't ask why they might need to feed her through it, or give her blood. I'd gone from being on autopilot to becoming locked in my own bubble.

It's 2020. There's nothing this hospital can't fix. Me and Daddy will help you, Azaylia. You are surrounded by all the love and care in the world. We are all here for you. You'll be better soon, princess.

I knew Ashley had been talking to his family and gathering information about leukaemia, but I didn't ask him what he had found out. I preferred to focus on the here and now. Azaylia was having this central line fitted so nobody would stick a needle in her again.

Let's get through that first.

'Would you both like to be with Azaylia when we sedate her?'

'Yes,' we told the nurse. 'Yes, of course.'

We wanted to know she was being handled with care. I trusted the doctors and nurses, don't get me wrong, but for my own peace of mind I had to be there, watching over my daughter. That was my job and she was my priority in life. I wanted her to hear my voice and know I hadn't left her alone, and Ashley felt the same way.

We were led along a corridor to a set of double doors, then another. Beyond the second set, we could see a team of medics standing around Azaylia's bed. They allowed us to stand beside her. She looked very poorly now, her face pasty white and still puffy, her eyes squished shut. She was very quiet too, just lying there in a nappy and a vest. She was so tiny and vulnerable, all I wanted was to scoop her into my arms and tell her how much we loved her, that everything was going to be alright.

The anaesthetist explained that Azaylia would be given gases to inhale to send her to sleep. This shocked me, the thought of it catapulting me back to being in labour.

Gas and air! I need it NOW PLEASE!

I could see myself writhing in pain, trying desperately to cope with the contractions. I was in agony, the gas and air barely touching the tips of the pain waves cascading through my body. Just eight weeks had passed since I gave birth to Azaylia. How were we in this situation? How could my baby be the one in a hospital bed?

The memories of my labour triggered a series of frightening thoughts about what Azaylia might be going through. *What if she was in pain? What if she was suffering? How long had she been poorly?* There were so many medics rushing around her. I stroked her head as the gas was wafted under her little nose. I asked them to do it that way, rather than put the mask straight over her face, and I was grateful they sedated her so delicately – it was the very least my precious little girl deserved.

We had to watch her go to theatre now and waited anxiously while Azaylia was having the surgery. Ashley had made more calls to the family, to let them know what was happening, but we still didn't discuss the diagnosis or the treatment between us. I was hiding in my own world, all my energy focused on what was happening to Azaylia right this minute and the fact we had to stay standing and be there for her when she came out of surgery.

What happened next completely floored us all over again. Azaylia had been slow to respond after her surgery, we were told, and she was going to be taken to intensive care.

Intensive care? Why? How is this happening?

'Only one of you is allowed in intensive care,' a nurse said. 'Who will it be?'

I broke down in tears. 'My poor baby!' I sobbed. 'How can she cope with all this?' Azaylia was a tiny little girl. She'd been through a massive trauma having the central line put in and the fact she needed to be in intensive care was utterly terrifying. I was panic-stricken at the idea of being split up from Ashley too: we were experiencing every parent's worst nightmare and we needed to support each other.

If anything happens to my baby, I thought, *I want to die.*

Me and Ashley immediately agreed that I would go into intensive care first and then we would swap. Almost before I could draw my next breath, a nurse was showing me the way.

My heart was pounding when we arrived at the big set of double doors leading into intensive care. There was a big nurses' desk in front of the doors and I followed the nurse past various bays and beds and rooms, all sectioned off from one another. The sterile smell and the *beep beep beep* and *ding ding ding* of all the machinery unnerved me. I glanced through the window of one room and saw a young child being cradled in his mother's arms. The little boy was unresponsive and his mum was bent around him on the bed, pain etched on her face. I felt so sorry for them; this was such a terrible place to be.

Azaylia was in a private room in the middle of the ward. I couldn't wait to see her, but my heart sank when I reached her cot. I didn't think Azaylia would look much different in here than she did before she went into surgery, but she did. She looked hot and bothered, yet she was somehow paler than before and she wasn't moving at all. It was frightening to see her like that. I was allowed to hold her hand and give her kisses, but she didn't respond in any way. I bent over the cot, whispering in her ear, telling her I loved her.

'I'm here, Azaylia,' I said, trying hard not to cry. 'When you wake up, I'm gonna give you such a big cuddle.'

I had a rattle in my handbag. It played music and lit up, and I gave it a little shake. 'Listen to this, Azaylia,' I told her. 'Are we going to play when you wake up, baby?'

I was struggling to hold myself together but I continued talking to Azaylia as calmly as I could. It seemed a natural thing to do, even though she couldn't hear me. When she started to come round, she would hear my voice and hopefully that would give her some comfort. That was all I could think about – I had to help make Azaylia feel as comfortable as possible. That was my job as her mum and it was my priority.

Azaylia needed her daddy too though, and me and Ashley needed to be together. It was preying on my mind that he wasn't in here with us and I didn't want to have to swap with him. The idea of it panicked me. How could I leave my baby's side at a time like this? That was what Ashley had been forced to do and it seemed so cruel and unfair.

There was a nurse in the room with me the whole time and I asked her if I could talk to the person in charge and explain that I wanted Ashley here: 'I'm scared,' I told her. 'We both are. What if something happens to our daughter and her daddy isn't here?' My plea was heard and I was told Ashley would be allowed to come and join us after all.

'Thank God,' I said, relief flooding through me.

. . .

Other nurses were coming and going all the time, constantly taking Azaylia's temperature and checking all the lines and wires attached to her. I didn't know what all these tubes were for and I didn't ask. This was a foreign land to me and I was incapable of taking all this in. I'd scarcely eaten since we arrived there the day before, I didn't know what day it was and I'd had no sleep. My brain felt numb and all I felt capable of doing was talking to Azaylia and stroking her face.

Ashley was here, finally. It was so good to see him, but it was incredibly painful too. 'Hello, princess,' he was saying. 'Are you gonna wake up soon? Are we gonna play?' He was reacting exactly the way I had, instinctively trying to be calm and positive around our daughter. I felt so much love for him.

I was half-hearing a lot of things now. Ashley was relaying news to his mum, my mum, his siblings and my brother, and they were passing news to everyone else. I'd spoke to a few family members too by now, though I did more listening than talking. 'She's gonna be OK,' our loved ones were saying.

'We're gonna get this sorted. She's in the best hands. She's a fighter. She's gonna get through this. Make sure you eat, you need to keep your energy up. Look after each other. How are you doing?'

How are you doing? That was a question that threw me. *Me?* I wasn't thinking about how I was doing, or how Ashley was doing. It wasn't about us, it was all about our little girl.

'If anything happens to Azaylia,' I told them, 'I don't want to live.'

That became my stock answer when anyone close asked me how I was. My fuzzy head might not be computing the details of Azaylia's condition and treatment, but I knew this was serious. People didn't know what to say when I talked like that. They repeated their positive messages and told us to make sure we looked after ourselves – 'Make sure you eat. Can we bring anything in? What about toiletries?' But I wasn't interested in food or clothes or cleaning my teeth. All we'd had to eat was packets of crisps and chocolate bars from the machine and we were still in the same set of clothes we arrived in.

When Azaylia eventually opened her eyes she stayed very still and looked around quietly, like a little doll coming to life. It was a big moment and it made my heart dance. She'd come out of her operation and, though she still needed to get her strength back, our baby was back.

'Hello, beautiful!'

Me and Ashley both made a big fuss of her, telling her what a strong and clever girl she was.

'I love you!' Ashley said. 'Daddy loves you! You're strong, baby, you're my Little Lion. I'm with you every step of the way.'

Little Lion, or 'lickle lion' as he liked to pronounce it. It was the first time I'd heard Ashley say that and it swelled my heart. It was the perfect nickname for Azaylia. She was strong and glorious and so magnificent, and she would fight like a lion – I knew she would.

I leaned over and gave her a kiss.

'Mummy and Daddy are sleeping by your cot tonight, yes we are!'

I felt a pang as I thought about our set-up at home, with Azaylia's little cot – one I'd taken so much time picking out and filling with the softest bedding – butted up next to our big double bed. It was the other way round now, with Azaylia's NHS cot taking centre stage and me and Ashley by her side.

I was only just starting to take in everything around us. We were in a place called PICU – the paediatric intensive care unit. It was where sick babies and children received the highest level of care. Our room was compact and functional. There was a piece of machinery above the cot that you could swing round. Everything Azaylia needed was attached to it, or attached to her, and there were lots of other machines beeping and bleeping all around. In the corner was a little red chair.

'You have it,' Ashley insisted.

'What about you?'

'I'll be fine. You're still recovering from the caesarean, you need it more than me.'

There was only one strip of empty floor, behind the base of the main piece of machinery. It would be just big enough for Ashley to lie down in, I thought. His brother Ryan sent in two rollout yoga mats as soon as he found out we were staying in and, when Ashley went to the coffee shop later that night, I made up a bed for him with some hospital sheets, blue covers and a pillow.

'I got you this,' Ashley said when he returned. He handed me a chicken and pesto panini and a chai latte. It was the first warm food I'd had in the hospital and I really appreciated it.

'Thank you,' I smiled. 'I made you a bed.'

We had a hug. There was no need for words – what would we say? It felt like we'd already exhausted the number of ways you could ask each other why and how we were. We knew we were there for each other and that was what counted.

That night, we took turns watching over Azaylia. Ashley managed to snatch some sleep, curled up on the yoga mats in his tracksuit, and I did my best to close my eyes in the chair, shuffling around when my abdomen felt sore and my back ached. I think I only managed seconds of sleep, that's how it felt. As soon as I heard Azaylia murmur, or one of the machines made a different sound, I shot out of my seat like a startled cat. 'What's this?' I'd say. 'Why's it doing that?' There was a nurse in the room, by our side, 24/7. They were all fantastic, always responding with lightning speed.

I lost track of whether it was night or day, and how long we had been in the hospital. Intensive care is like that – it was as if we'd entered a parallel universe.

'Does Mum want a cuddle?' a nurse asked.

'Can I? Really?'

The last time Azaylia had been in my arms was when I lifted her out of her car seat and handed her to my mum. It felt like an age ago and I was desperate to hold her close to me.

The nurse lifted her out of the cot, careful not to dislodge any of the wires attached to her little body. I was positioned in the red chair, ready to hold my daughter again, at last. If Ashley had held her like she was a porcelain doll when she was a newborn, Azaylia was now made of the finest glass. I was terrified of knocking a tube or a wire out of place, but as soon as she was lying in my arms my fears retreated. I was so happy and relieved to hold my baby again and I was swamped with feelings of the most intense love.

I settled Azaylia in the crook of my left arm. She was swaddled in a blanket and seemed comfortable, despite the wires and tabs all over her. I stared at her for a long time, taking in each tiny eyelash, every soft hair on her head, every pore on her pretty nose. Her skin was rosy and so clear now, her eyes were fully open again. Best of all there was light in her eyes – I could see it shining.

'You're amazing, Azaylia,' I told her.

She gurgled and waved her little hands around. They were tucked inside mittens, to stop her pulling at the wires. I'd bought her several pairs of scratch mittens, having been told that little babies can scratch themselves with their tiny shell-like fingernails. Never in a million years did I think they'd have another use.

The nurse was explaining that the machines were monitoring things like Azaylia's heart rate, breathing and blood pressure. Some of the wires could be unclipped for short periods of time – when she needed a wash, for instance – but the central line must never come out. The nurse described it as a 'lollipop system', with green wires being OK to remove and the red ones having to stay in place all the time. I still didn't ask what treatment she was going to have, or what fluid or medicine would go down the central line. Azaylia was so small and delicate, so pure and innocent. I didn't have the mental capacity to process what was happening, or was going to happen next to her little body.

Doctors were coming and going now too. Readings were taken, conversations had, wires checked and tubes detached and re-attached. The more I started to take in what each wire was doing, the more comfortable I felt when I held Azaylia. Still, I continued to sit like a statue when she was in my arms, just in case I jolted something out of place. I didn't even shift position when my fingertips prickled with pins and needles and the whole of my left arm went numb. It could fall off for all I cared. I had Azaylia with me, she was comfortable and all her wires were in the right place – that was what was important.

'Mum, you need to put her back in.'

I'd dozed off and the nurse was there in an instant, making sure Azaylia was safe. I knew she was safe – she was in my arms, and I would never let her fall.

• • •

The next day we were shown how to wash Azaylia, using a little bowl of water, a wash lotion called Octenisan and Conti wipes, which were like disposable wash cloths. Ashley and I did it together, talking to Azaylia softly as we cleaned her little body – 'There you are, princess. Don't you look a pretty girl now? Aren't you all fresh and beautiful?'

She was looking at us, just like she used to, and it really felt like we'd turned a corner. We'd been on the sidelines for days, watching the professionals care for our daughter. This was the first time we had been able to really do something for her and it felt so bonding and comforting. I enjoyed it. I looked at Ashley, wanting to acknowledge this small pleasure with a smile or a positive word, but when I saw his face my heart sank. He looked broken and he looked scared. It knocked the breath out of my lungs. He's such a strong guy, the man who's branded himself as 'The Beast', because he's incredibly tough and strong and fighting fit. It was devastating to see him like that, but I didn't address it. I couldn't bring myself to and what would I say?

My eyes were already back on Azaylia. She still had bruising on her tummy, which hadn't gone down at all. They needed to get her white cell count down. That was why she had the central line put in, so she could be given the treatment she needed.

'Open wide, Azaylia!' Ashley said. 'Good girl! I'm just going to give your mouth a little wash, princess.'

He was smiling at her, putting on a happy show for his baby. I could feel his energy lift as he spoke to her and it lifted mine too. This is what Azaylia needed – she had to be surrounded with love and positivity.

We'd been given small pink sponges that looked like lollipops on sticks. A nurse showed us how to make up a dilution of Chlorhexidine mouthwash and water in a dappen dish, then gently work the sponge around the inside of Azaylia's mouth. Ashley told Azaylia exactly what he was going to do and she looked as though she listened to every word. She was such a good girl, lying still while we took turns in making sure we'd cleaned every corner of her mouth.

Her baby hair was so delicate and fine, and I started to use the sponges to wash her hair too, making S shapes through it and then combing the back bits round. I loved to see Azaylia so clean and cared for, her face all washed and her hair all done.

She's a fighter like her daddy, I told myself. *She's a survivor like her mum.*

'Look at you, champ! Let's go!'

CHAPTER
SEVEN

Azaylia was unsettled and she started giving little cries. 'What's the matter, baby? Do you want to listen to your music?' I said.

I switched the lights on her favourite rattle and sang along to the nursery rhymes it played. She normally loved it, following the lights with her eyes, but she wasn't interested at all.

Ashley was on the phone to his brother and other family members. He wanted to know more about the type of leukaemia Azaylia had been diagnosed with. She had AML, which stood for Acute Myeloid Leukaemia. That's what had caused her white blood cell count to be as high as 200. A healthy person's white blood cell count is around five and adults who are suffering from leukaemia tend to have a white blood cell count way lower than 200, Ashley was hearing.

I didn't need to hear it, and I didn't want to hear it. Azaylia was going to get out of intensive care and then she was going to come home with us. If you'd asked me at the time, I'd have struggled to repeat what AML even stood for.

Now her central line was in place, and her temperature was no longer spiking, Azaylia was going to be treated to have her white blood cell count reduced. I didn't know how exactly, because I still wasn't asking any medical questions. All I wanted to know was what I could do for my baby to make her more comfortable right now. Had her nappy been changed? Did I need to wash her face? Did she need a clean vest? They were practical things I could do for Azaylia.

I couldn't compute any of the things Ashley was hearing. About 3,000 people a year are diagnosed with AML, he was told. The risk of getting it increases with age and Azaylia was one of about 100 children a year given the diagnosis.

It's so rare, I thought. *How will she cope?*

Azaylia was still unsettled so I spoke to her in a sing-songy voice, like I always had at home. I stroked her cheek and put my face close to hers. She usually grabbed my hair and gurgled, but nothing was working today.

I kept an 'emergency' dummy for Azaylia. The kind of emergency I'd bought it for was if she was screaming in a supermarket and I couldn't soothe her any other way. I'd given it to my mum when we went to Manchester and Azaylia had had it that day.

I fished it out of her bag now and thought how silly of me not to have thought of giving it to Azaylia sooner.

'Is she allowed it in here?' I asked the nurse.

She was, and the nurse gave me a little pot with Sweet-Ease in it, to dip the dummy in, explaining it was a sucrose and purified water solution used to calm and soothe distressed infants.

'Do you want your dummy, Azaylia? Do you?'

Azaylia immediately started sucking on the dummy. She was like Maggie from *The Simpsons*, chomping away like it was her favourite food ever.

'Good girl!' I said. 'Look, Ashley, look how she loves her dummy!'

The frowns etched on his face when he talked on the phone were immediately replaced with smiles as he told Azaylia what a clever girl she was. And she *was* clever, very quickly learning that if she spat the dummy out and had a little cry, Daddy would dip it in the sweet-tasting water again.

'Do you want some more?' he said straight away. 'OK, baby, Daddy will do your dummy for you, Azaylia.'

She'd had him round her little finger from the day she was born and nothing had changed.

'Ashley, don't keep falling for it!' I said. 'I don't want her having so much sugar.'

It would be months before Azaylia moved onto solids, I thought, and I didn't want her hooked on a sugary taste before I even started weaning her.

'OK, OK,' he said, but as soon as Azaylia gave him her puppy dog eyes and had another little whimper, the dummy was dipped in the sugary water again and Maggie from *The Simpsons* was back.

'How can I say no?' Ashley said every time. 'Look at her little face! Here you go, princess.'

As the hours turned into days, me and Ashley watched over Azaylia constantly, only leaving the room to go to the toilet or the shop, or to talk to family members who were desperate for news. I ate and drank only out of necessity, simply to exist and to have enough energy to watch over Azaylia. I said my prayers regularly, as I always did at home, but they were very different now.

Towards the end of my pregnancy there had been days when I felt low and frustrated. I moaned at Ashley for not doing enough around the house and I was annoyed at him for not giving me a massage when he knew my back was aching, even though I didn't ask him to. I also prayed for lockdown to end so we could return to some sort of normality, but all of those thoughts and niggles seemed so trivial now, I didn't know what real problems were. My only prayer now was for my baby to get better and to come home as quickly as possible.

'You OK, Safiyya?' Ashley asked. He asked the same question routinely, whenever he'd nipped out and then came back into Azaylia's room.

'Yeah, fine. You?'

'Yeah, good.'

Whenever I had to leave the room I'd feel the tears and panic rising to the surface, but every time I returned to Azaylia's bedside, I was in control again. It was as if some kind of survival mode cartridge was planted inside me.

Putting on a strong front and being on autopilot was the only way we could function. Ashley looked lost and tired and so scared, but he wasn't breaking down. I was the same. I wanted to fall to my knees, but my head knew I had to stand up, for Azaylia's sake. She needed both of us there, as solid as we could be. Talking about our emotions would have opened the floodgates and I instinctively felt we couldn't risk filling Azaylia's room with tears.

. . .

'We're moving Azaylia onto the ward.'

Relief lapped at my heart. Azaylia had been in intensive care for five days and I'd never felt so grateful for news. I thanked the doctor and immediately went to tell Azaylia what was happening.

'We're moving out of intensive care, baby! Well done! You're amazing, Azaylia. I knew you could do it!'

She was in good spirits, looking very responsive and giving me eye contact. An ordinary ward seemed a much better place for her to be, now she was holding her own so much better.

'We'd better start packing up your things, baby!'

I realised Ashley had stayed very quiet and, when I glanced over at him, I saw he looked shell-shocked.

'This is good news, babe,' I said. 'It's a really positive move forward.'

'I know, Safiyya,' he said. He was happy we were moving out of intensive care, but even so he sounded lethargic and worn down. This wasn't a time to punch the air and celebrate. After all, Azaylia wasn't being discharged and she still had to undergo treatment to wipe the leukaemia out of her body. We both got that, even though moving to the ward could only be a good sign.

I didn't understand what this treatment would be. 'Leukae-mia' was still a very foreign word to me and I had no more understanding of it than I had when Azaylia was first given the diagnosis. One of the doctors had advised us not to look online but instead to speak to her if we wanted to know anything, so that the information we got was accurate. I accepted that and I didn't look anything up, but nor did I ask questions. Later on, before we left intensive care, the same specialist took me aside and explained things to me in simple terms. I don't know if she recognised that I wasn't absorbing information or asking ques-tions, but however it came about, I really appreciated the time she took with me.

She told me to imagine that the white blood cells are white cars and the red blood cells are red cars: 'Azaylia has 200 hundred white cars and three red cars in her blood. The red cars can't get past the white cars. There's so many white cars, it's like the red cars are stuck.'

I listened intently, taking it all in.

'The red cars are the ones carrying oxygen,' she went on, 'and unless we get rid of some of the white cars, the oxygen can't be carried around the body the way it needs to be. So that's what we need to do. We need to get rid of lots of the white cars, because there are far too many of them.'

The explanation really helped me to understand what had gone wrong in Azaylia's body or, more precisely, in her blood. I had so many more questions trying to claw their way up from the pit of my stomach and into my brain.

How long will it take to get rid of the white cells? Could they come back? How do you take them out of her blood?

I wasn't ready to ask them yet. I had enough to process for the time being and I was afraid to hear the answers.

. . .

Azaylia was being moved onto Ward 18, which I understood was a children's ward. Nurses were leading the way, pushing her in a cot on wheels as me and Ashley walked alongside. Our daughter was sleeping soundly in the centre of the convoy, oblivious to it all. She looked content and rosy-skinned, and I was so pleased to see that. The improvement since she was admitted to intensive care was very clear to see. Her journey was taking her in the right direction, that's how it felt.

There was a plaster on one of her little cheeks, holding down the tube that led into her nose. This was called an NG line, I'd learned, short for 'naso-gastric', and it was the tube Azaylia was fed down. When she was brought in, she had been too weak and poorly to drink from a bottle, or to be breastfed. My body seemed to chime in, without me really noticing, because it was only now that I realised the initial pains I felt from having engorged breasts had already subsided. It was a physical relief not to be producing milk that wasn't needed, but emotionally it hurt. I'd loved the bond I felt with Azaylia when I was feeding her and I would have carried on for longer, but so what? My feelings didn't come into it. Azaylia needed to be properly nourished, so that was the end of it.

The corridors were empty because of Covid restrictions and the sound of the wheels clacking on the hard floor echoed loudly around my ears. I didn't know the layout of the hospital and I kept thinking we were going to arrive on the ward any minute now, but then another corridor would open up, and another. It was like walking through an alien world and the further we walked, the more I started to feel like I was in somebody else's body, entering someone else's life.

I'd never been on a children's ward before but I imagined it would be a haven at the end of this eerie labyrinth. There would be bright-coloured furniture, pictures on the walls and toys to play with. The sound of children's voices would replace the ominous *beep beep beep* and *ding ding ding* of the intensive care ward and, best of all, when you heard nurses racing to a bedside in the middle of the night, you wouldn't wonder if the very worst was happening.

When I finally stepped into Ward 18 the brightness of the lights dazzled me. We'd had the blinds down in our room on intensive care and I'd got used to the soft dimness. I blinked and blinked again, and then suddenly I felt like I had no stability in my body. The floor had become water. I couldn't feel my fingers or my toes, my face was numb. As I floated down the ward I was seeing children with no hair and no eyebrows. I'd seen children who looked like this on the TV, but never in real life. There was a boy aged about ten walking towards us. He had no hair and he was pushing a metal frame alongside him, with two bags attached to it.

We're on the wrong ward, I thought. *This is a mistake. Why are we here?*

I looked at the doctors and nurses around me. *What are we doing here? What's going on?* I could see myself searching their faces for answers, which was the strangest sensation. They were all wearing masks and so I was hunting in their eyes for answers, but there weren't any and nobody was speaking. My own words felt muzzled inside my mouth. If I tried to speak, I was sure I'd make no sound.

There were lots of cubicles and beds, all with tape around them. It was a reminder to keep to the two-metre social distancing rule that was in place because of Covid, just as I had in the maternity hospital. Through a gap in a curtain I glimpsed a little girl wearing a headscarf. Her mother was sitting beside her, reading her a book. I kept floating down the ward, the snapshots into other families' worlds blurring in my head. Wires and tubes, bald heads, oxygen cylinders and pale faces. They were everywhere I looked and I felt terrified.

The young boy was closer now. He was wearing brightly coloured pyjamas and I could see that he had an NG tube attached to his nose. Unexpectedly, a big smile appeared on his face as he waved at the nurses. *He's happy!* I thought, relief flooding through me. *We're going to be OK here, after all.*

Azaylia was having a room of her own, rather than a cubicle on the more open sections of the ward. That was because she was a baby and had come from intensive care, I assumed. Unlike the old-fashioned corridors that led us here, there was nothing remotely eerie about this part of the hospital. The ward had recently been refurbished and Azaylia's room was big and modern and airy. There was a large blue and green cot bed in the centre of the room, a TV on the wall and little sets of blue and white cabinets on wheels to put our things in. Best of all, a huge window looked out onto a seating area that was lit with lots of different-coloured lights. As she settled Azaylia into her cot, a nurse explained that the lights looked lovely, especially in the evening. They were sensory lights, she said, and all the children liked to look out of their rooms and watch them changing colour.

'There's a new shower and bathroom area you can use,' she went on. 'And this chair is for you.'

There was one chair in the room. It was covered in red faux leather and looked much more comfortable than the plastic chair I'd been sleeping in all week, but my heart constricted when I looked at it.

We'd had it explained to us that only one parent at a time was allowed to stay on this ward because of the strict Covid rules. The family had already booked us a room at the hotel opposite, which was open to hospital visitors. One of us would stay there and we would take it in turns to stay with Azaylia. We had no idea how long she would be in hospital, but one of us would be at her side always.

Ashley had volunteered to do the first night in the hotel and he had to leave now. He didn't want to leave and I didn't want him to go. We'd been like one parent joined together in here: we worked around each other, we understood one another. We didn't need to speak or ask questions. Just being in the same room gave us strength and support.

'I love you, baby,' Ashley said, giving Azaylia a kiss.

She was wide awake now and she looked him straight in the eye and batted his face with a mitten-covered hand. I'm sure if she could talk she would have said 'I love you too'. The situation felt so confusing. If she hadn't had the NG tube stuck to her cheek, you wouldn't have known there was anything wrong with her. She was puffy in the face and she was tired and lethargic, but even so she looked as beautiful as the day she was born.

Ashley was trying to be practical and positive, talking about the family members who were bringing food and fresh clothes and toiletries to the hotel for us. Everybody was supporting us and he said he would bring me anything I needed when he came back the next day. I didn't have to worry about anything outside this hospital room because everything was being taken care of.

We stared at each other for a moment. I didn't need to be told not to think about anything outside this room, I thought. Nothing existed outside of this room. It was the same for Ashley.

'Can I have a dressing gown, please?' I said, as an afterthought.

• • •

Unbelievably, I was still wearing the same clothes I'd travelled to Manchester in several days before. It would be amazing to have something comfortable to put on, I thought, because when I held Azaylia I wanted her to have something snuggly to cuddle up to.

After we hugged goodbye I watched Ashley walk away. It felt very surreal, like we were actors being forced to play roles. We hadn't chosen to be in this scene and we were struggling to connect with the characters we had become, but the curtain was already up and we had no choice but to keep going.

I was the sole parent in charge of Azaylia now and it felt like a very lonely place to be. There were nurses coming in and out all the time, but they were so covered in protective clothing because of Covid I had trouble distinguishing one from the other. They were all very kind and dedicated, talking to me about Azaylia's new routine and trying to help me settle in, but they were very busy too and their priority was to get all of their jobs done as efficiently as possible.

'You can use these cupboards for your things. Azaylia's clothes and nappies can go in here ...'

There was so much to take in, and without Ashley, it felt like my responsibilities had doubled. Azaylia needed Mummy to listen and learn, and I didn't want to miss anything at all.

'The Oramorph will be in a syringe. The doctor will come and talk to you ...'

I was concentrating hard but their voices were vibrating round the room, the information bouncing off me. *Oramorph?* Had I heard that wrong? That was morphine. I knew it was morphine. But by the time that information filtered through to my brain, the nurse had gone.

I sat on the edge of the red chair and told myself I would ask the next nurse who came in about Azaylia's medication.

Everything was fine, everything was under control. For the first time, I had a proper look around the room. As well as the new furniture and the TV and the window with the pretty lights, there were all sorts of machines around Azaylia's cot. I had no idea what most were for, but I did recognise one piece of equipment: it was an oxygen tank, on the wall.

Why do we need all this? I thought. *Why isn't this just a basic bed area? Did they put us here because there's no space anywhere else in the hospital? Or was it that they didn't want to put Azaylia on the cancer part of the ward?*

CHAPTER
EIGHT

I was walking on water again, but this time cold air was biting at my throat. The noise of the traffic was incredibly loud. It was like having the worst hangover ever and everybody is screaming in your ears and flashing lights in your eyes. I pulled my dressing gown tight across my chest as I flicked my head around to look at the hospital behind me. It took all my strength not to turn back and run to Azaylia.

Daddy is with her now. They have everything they need. You have to go and get some rest.

I scoured all the windows of the hospital, trying to work out if I could see the one that belonged to Azaylia's ward. How were they getting on in there? Before Ashley came across from the hotel I'd spent ages organising the cupboards, so if he couldn't find anything I'd be able to tell him exactly where all her things were. Nappies, dummies, vests, toys, rattles, wipes, creams. I didn't want him to have to wait to ask a nurse for help. Azaylia

needed to be as comfortable as possible all the time, and everything had to be to hand immediately.

I'd waited until the very last moment to leave her, holding
her in my arms and telling her Mummy would be back soon and
that Daddy was coming to look after her. I didn't want to let go,
not even so I could put on some clothes. It was only when Ashley
phoned to tell me he was at the hospital entrance that I finally
put Azaylia back in her cot, kissed her little forehead and dashed
downstairs, as fast as my legs would take me.

'How is she?' Ashley was scouring my face.

'Good. She's good.'

He looked so stressed, despite the fact he'd had some sleep
in the hotel.

'Great,' he said. 'Thanks. You're doing great, Safiyya. Go and
get some rest. Azaylia needs you to look after yourself, yeah?'

We had a quick hug and ran in opposite directions. The
nurses were tending to her every need, but even so neither of us
wanted to leave Azaylia without a parent at her bedside. Ashley
didn't comment on the fact I wasn't dressed properly, though I
must have looked crazy, walking outside and crossing the road in
my dressing gown on a bitterly cold October day. My hands and
feet were numb with cold, but the rest of my body was spiking
with adrenaline. It felt like the only thing that was fuelling me
forward. Without it, I think I'd have fallen to the side of the road.

The moment I walked in the hotel room I wanted to collapse
on the floor. I felt frozen from the inside out, through cold,
exhaustion and so much distress. I was desperate to have a shower,

to warm me through and bring me back to life, and the very first thing I did was walk into the bathroom.

Feeling the warm water soak through my hair was so comforting and luxurious. It was as if I'd never experienced a shower in my life before. I savoured every drop of water running down my face and over every inch of my skin. It was as if my whole body was wrapped up in a huge, warm cuddle. I stayed in the shower for a very long time, until I felt heated to the core and the bathroom was like a steam room.

The family had brought food and clean clothes and all the toiletries we could possibly need. I pulled on a pair of fresh cotton pyjamas and climbed straight into bed. It was such a relief to be able to lie down flat after so many days of sitting cramped up in a chair, worrying about whether Azaylia was comfortable in my arms or whether I was doing any damage to my caesarean scar. I stretched out my arms and felt the weight of my body sink into the mattress – *like a ton of bricks*, I thought.

When I woke up the next morning, that thought was the last thing I could remember. *I feel like a ton of bricks.* I must have fallen asleep a second after it went through my mind.

You aren't dreaming, this is real. You're in a hotel and you need to get to the hospital.

That was my very next thought and it snatched at my breath. I still felt like a ton of bricks, but I had to get up and go back to Azaylia. My adrenaline kicked back in as soon as I lifted my head off the pillow. My mind was racing now and I was up and on the phone to Ashley in a flash, asking how Azaylia had slept and whether I needed to bring anything for her. After getting myself ready at breakneck speed, I was on my way back to the hospital as quickly as humanly possible. This hotel was just a service station, here to clean us and fuel us and power us up, ready to go again.

When I reached the hospital entrance I had a very powerful sensation: a different body was waiting for me at the door. That's what I felt, and I stepped into it without hesitation. Straight away, I was back into robotic mummy mode – I was here to serve Azaylia and my emotions would have to take a back seat.

We had a meeting with a specialist today. Though we couldn't both be at Azaylia's side at the same time, me and Ashley were allowed to attend meetings together. This one was going to be about the course of treatment Azaylia was having and we were meeting at a doctor's office.

I arrived first and sat down to wait for Ashley, feeling irritated and frustrated. I didn't want to be sitting outside a doctor's office – I wanted to be with Azaylia, in her room. I didn't want to miss a minute of my time with her, but we'd agreed to swap over after this meeting and I had to be patient.

Breathe. You will see your baby soon, and the nurses will be with her when Ashley comes down.

It was incredibly quiet in this waiting area, though inside my head the noise level was rising fast. I couldn't turn it down. It was as if all the scary things I'd been told and all the frightening words I'd heard over the past week were tired of being pushed away. They were tunnelling under my scalp and inside my skull, shouting and fighting as they marched on to the front of my brain and knocked on it loudly, demanding to be heard. It was terrifying and I put my hands over my ears and clenched my jaw to stop myself from crying out.

'You OK, Safiyya?'

Hearing Ashley's voice made me jump, but I was so glad to see him. The war in my head was interrupted and I snapped back into automatic mode.

'Yeah!' I said. 'All good. You?'

'Yeah, good,' he said. 'Guess what?'

'What?'

'The moment I opened my eyes this morning, I looked over my shoulder to see if Azaylia was awake. And you know what?'

'What?'

'She was lying there quietly, wide awake, and as soon as she saw me she gave me the biggest smile.'

'Wow,' I said. 'That's so beautiful!'

I looked at Ashley and felt so much love in my heart. He was a week ahead of me, I realised. The battle in my brain had forced me to see things as they really were. Ashley hadn't shrunk and hidden from Azaylia's diagnosis like I had. Right from the start, he had been talking to his family about exactly what leukaemia was. He had been confronting the truth so bravely while I shut myself in my bubble, busying myself with nappies and babygros and desperately positive thoughts. It was so much easier to be in the moment because the future – tomorrow – next month – next year – was absolutely terrifying. But Ashley had been facing the truth head on, right from day one. The family had been supporting him. His loved ones had been on the phone, helping him understand Azaylia's diagnosis, but even so, he must have felt so alone, and so scared.

Our little girl had a rare and aggressive type of cancer, that was the truth of it. There was no getting away from that and it was time to face the reality in all its horror, just as Ashley had.

This appointment was with the oncologist and it was about the chemotherapy Azaylia was having, not just to get rid of the glut of white blood cells, but to tackle the tumours in her body. I hadn't been able to verbalise this fact, or process it in any way, but this was the reality. Azaylia had tumours in her stomach, lungs and kidneys. She'd had scans and we'd been given the results days and days ago, though I couldn't remember who told us, or how. It was like trying to see faces in a smoke-filled room, or listen to ghosts whispering in the wind.

The news was too horrific, too unbelievable. *This couldn't be happening to my little girl, could it?*

The fact was they had started giving her chemotherapy in intensive care and her treatment was continuing on Ward 18. I'd been told this already, but I'd been pushing against it. If I talked about lumps and bruises instead of tumours, it was far less terrifying. It was easier to say Azaylia was on a children's ward, not a ward for children with cancer. She had 'too many white blood cells' in her body, not a rare and aggressive type of blood cancer. And when I started to hear that she needed chemotherapy, I called it medicine or treatment, because it was easier to stomach. I knew chemo was used to treat cancer, but I didn't allow myself to make the link from Azaylia's chemo to cancer. *Do you use chemo to treat other conditions? You must do.* That's how my mind was working.

I didn't make a conscious decision to dilute the words and I wasn't deliberately trying to hide from reality. My head played tricks without my permission and perhaps that was for the best? The unfiltered truth about Azaylia's diagnosis was so brutal and shocking it would have knocked me off my feet.

I had nowhere to hide now.

The oncologist showed us into a side room and Ashley and I sat rigid in our seats, waiting to hear what would happen next.

I knew this was not going to be an easy conversation; I knew enough about chemotherapy to know how powerful it was and how sick it could make you. I'd seen the children with bald heads on the ward and I tried not to think about Azaylia losing her precious cap of baby hair. She had a huge collection of hairbands and I loved putting them on her. It was a good thing she was used to them, I thought. She looked so pretty in them and she would still look beautiful if she lost her hair – I'd make sure of that.

When the oncologist started to speak I felt the shift in me. I was fully switched on and I wanted to know everything I possibly could about Azaylia's ongoing treatment. How much chemo would she still need to have? How long would she be on it? How much longer would she have to be in hospital?

I asked the oncologist if I could record the meeting, so I could listen again if I wanted to double-check anything. It would also be good to be able to send the recording to close family, so that nothing was lost in translation and we didn't have to repeat the information again and again. The oncologist agreed and I pressed 'record' on my phone and listened intently as the procedure was explained.

Azaylia was going to continue to receive her chemotherapy in liquid form over several days. It would be bright blue in colour and it would drip-feed into the central line in her chest, taking about half an hour to get into her system. She might have two different types of chemo, one in the morning and one in the evening.

'What's the next step?'

I was hungry for facts and wanted to know every last detail. Azaylia would have a few weeks off after completing her chemo, so the whole 'round', as it was known, would take about a month.

There so was much to learn and I wanted to educate myself as much as possible.

'How does the chemotherapy actually cure the leukaemia?' I asked.

The oncologist was fantastic, using simple language to explain how the chemotherapy would attack the leukaemia cells. But she didn't use the word cure, I noticed, and I picked up on that straight away.

'The chemotherapy will work, won't it?' I asked, searching her face. 'It will cure her?'

The oncologist was very honest with us. Azaylia's cancer was extremely aggressive. She had tumours all around her body and, when the leukaemia cells were attacked by the chemo, her little body might not be able to take it.

'You mean, the chemotherapy could take her?'

The oncologist nodded. 'It's a possibility, I'm afraid.'

I couldn't believe what I was hearing. I thought I'd got this. I'd geared myself up to be super strong for Azaylia – I wouldn't shy away from any of the facts about chemotherapy, I'd educate myself and then I'd be in the best possible position to support her through the treatment. I was totally unprepared for the fact the treatment itself could kill her and the images this planted in my mind were so upsetting. I could see the cancer cells popping and bursting inside her little body, and Azaylia not being strong enough to endure it.

'If the chemo is successful, what happens then?'

Ashley was asking questions and I forced myself to stay focused and positive, like he was.

'Will she have to have a second round of chemo?' he asked.

The oncologist said it would be a question of waiting to see what affect the chemo had on Azaylia's leukaemia count. She might be given another round of chemo, if she was strong enough to take it.

'She's strong,' I heard Ashley say. 'She'll get through the chemo. Her leukaemia count will be knocked down to zero, I guarantee it. She's a little soldier. Look how far she's come already.'

When we left the room, I started sobbing uncontrollably and Ashley had tears pouring down his cheeks.

'I'm going straight to the ward to see Azaylia,' I cried. I felt like falling to my knees, but I was desperate to hold her and tell her how much I loved her, and I started marching down the corridor.

'Safiyya,' he said, his voice cracking. 'You can't let Azaylia see you like this.'

I turned to look at him. I'd never seen him look so crushed and scared, but there was passion and determination in his voice.

'You CANNOT let Azaylia see you like this,' he repeated.

'I know,' I said, stopping in my tracks as I remembered the pact we'd made back in intensive care. 'You're right.'

When Azaylia was in intensive care, Ashley had spoken passionately one day about the fact that we needed to stay positive around her.

'Babies can't speak but they are very sensory beings,' he had said. 'They pick up on things, probably more than we do. Azaylia is an amazing little girl. She has one of the rarest and most aggressive forms of cancer. If we hadn't brought her in when we did, we could have woken up one day and she wouldn't have woken up with us. But look at her now! Look how she's fighting! She's brave and she's strong and we have to be as positive and fearless as she is.'

It was a shock to hear it all spelled out like that, but I knew he was right and I listened to every world Ashley said.

'Azaylia *cannot* see us cry,' he continued. 'She *cannot* see us upset. She *cannot* see us having a bad day.'

He declared that, whenever we were in the room with Azaylia, it was 'Club 100' – 'We bring 100 per cent happy, positive energy. We smile, we dance, we play. We put music on, we surround our daughter with good vibes and we make every day as joyful as we possibly can. When she has her chemotherapy, Azaylia is going to fight like a lion. She is going to rise to the challenge. She is going to defeat this cancer and she is going to WIN. We need to show her that we believe in her and we need to surround her with nothing but love and joy and positive energy.'

I wiped the tears from my cheeks. Remembering Ashley's brave words also reminded me of all the reasons I fell in love with him. To listen to him was so inspiring and I admired him so much. I agreed with everything he said about Club 100. It made perfect sense. Our daughter was going to fight and she was going to survive. There was no question of that and we would not show a single crack in our armour as we supported her through her battle.

• • •

'Azaylia! Guess who's here? It's Mummy! Are we going to have a cuddle? Shall we get you all clean and fresh before playtime?'

My princess was dressed in a pretty white sleepsuit with a giraffe on that said 'I love my mummy' and she looked so happy and full of expectation. My heart went out to her. If she could talk, I'm sure she'd have said, 'Hey, Mummy, it's so good to see you! How are you doing? I've had lots of fun with Daddy, you know. What are we going to play today?'

The tumours made her uncomfortable. That was why she was being given Oramorph, to help her cope with the pain, though you would never have known what she was going through. Lying in her cot, she gurgled and smiled at me with her eyes. Azaylia wasn't just grabbing at life, she was doing everything she could to connect with me and spread her infectious energy. She was an absolute inspiration and she made it easier than I could have hoped for to leave my fears and heartache at the door. All I had to do was match her energy and joy, and it was all for her, so how could I fail?

That night we looked at the sensory lights through the window of her room. I cradled Azaylia in my arms and talked to her about all the lovely colours we could see, and I played music on my phone, singing songs to her and telling her how beautiful she was. Whitney Houston's 'When You Believe' was our favourite, I loved singing it to her and she always responded.

When she drifted off to sleep I laid her in her cot and sat myself down in the red chair, thinking about the day and what Ashley said about Club 100. I watched her chest slowly rise and fall and her eyelids twitch as she dreamt, and I realised I was still smiling at her, even though Azaylia couldn't see me. I was exhausted and my bones were aching, but Azaylia's strength had rubbed off on me and it was keeping me from sinking.

When she was in intensive care, Ashley put up a post on his Instagram, sharing the news. I wasn't sure about doing this at first, thinking it would be better to tell everyone later on, once we were out of hospital and Azaylia was well again. But Ashley's phone had been going mad with work calls. People were wondering where he was, why he'd suddenly dropped off the grid and how come his social media accounts had ground to a halt. He didn't have the time or the headspace to get back to everyone individually and the Instagram post was his way of letting everyone know at once what was happening. I understood that and gave him my blessing, and I'm glad I did. Thinking about it now, I realised it had done more than just share the news. It had brought in love and support, which is exactly what we wanted in Club 100.

I picked up my phone and re-read the post: 'Yesterday I had to go through something no parent in the world should have to go through,' Ashley had written. 'The single most upsetting, terrifying and heartbreaking experience I have ever been through.' After sharing Azaylia's diagnosis he asked people to say a prayer for her. 'Mummy and Daddy love you, princess,' he said, signing off with 'Let's go, champ' and 'You CAN and you WILL beat this!' He added a video of himself giving Azaylia a motivational talk as she lay on her side in her cot, sucking on her dummy. 'We are going to challenge this and we are going to succeed. And we're going to do it together.'

I drank in every second of that video and it melted my heart. I felt so proud of Ashley for his attitude and the way he was facing this. He was the best daddy Azaylia could wish for and he was doing everything in his power to match her spirit and energy and support her through this.

I could see that tens of thousands of people had read the post and viewed the video, and there was an avalanche of support from all around the world. I started reading some of the comments. Ashley's followers were telling us to be strong and that we were amazing parents. They were all sending love and so many positive thoughts to our beautiful little girl. I was blown away by the response. I hadn't expected this at all. Social media gets such a bad press at times, but Ashley's post had provoked nothing but positivity.

Azaylia needed all the love and support we could give her and, if Instagram buoyed us up, bring it on. We needed every drop of positivity we could get.

CHAPTER
NINE

'Aren't you the prettiest pumpkin I ever did see?'

Azaylia was kicking her legs as she lay in her cot, smiling up at me. She was dressed in an adorable orange pumpkin outfit, complete with a collar of green leaves and a floppy orange hat. I'd spent hours decorating her room with spooky spiders and Halloween balloons. Orange fairy lights twinkled around her cot and hanging off the rails at the foot of her mattress was a big white-faced witch. Club 100 was in full swing and had been for the past couple of weeks, as Azaylia was given her chemotherapy.

She'd had a catheter put in to begin with and I'd watch the bright blue medicine coming out of her body afterwards. We'd been warned that her urine would be toxic and that we mustn't let it touch our skin. That sent a chill through my veins. My precious little baby had this incredibly powerful medicine dripping into her body for thirty minutes, twice a day, for days and days. When I was pregnant I'd been so careful about what

I ate. I nourished myself with good, clean food, knowing I was nourishing my baby too. I cooked from scratch, making healthy dishes with fresh chicken and organic rice and vegetables, and I'd already started to read up on how to wean my baby with all the best nutritious foods. Now she was being pumped full of the most poisonous concoctions of drugs, because that was the only chance she had of getting better. It was very hard to take in.

I always said my prayers before Azaylia had her chemo. 'The medicine is here to protect and heal you,' I said, silently asking Allah or God to look after my baby girl and to give her the strength to keep fighting like the little soldier she was.

I was brought up around both Islam and Christianity, and ever since I was a child I've dipped in and out of both religions, unsure exactly what I believed. I've always believed in a God though – perhaps one God with two names? – and as I grew up, I became a firm believer that if you are a good person on earth you receive goodness back and you earn your place in heaven.

'Please make Azaylia well,' I prayed. 'She is a beautiful, pure soul. Please, please help her. Look at her. She is fighting so hard, she is fighting with so much grace and dignity too. She never complains. She deserves to live a beautiful life.'

I always sat beside Azaylia when she had her chemo, holding her hand and stroking her head. There were many times when I had to stop myself imagining what was going on underneath her lovely soft skin. If my mind insisted on dragging me there, I'd try very hard to focus on the cancer and the tumours, and how they were being zapped away, rather than any damage that might be happening inside the rest of her little body. It wasn't always easy. One day I had to turn my face from hers so she didn't see me bite my lip and wipe away my tears. I'd been looking into Azaylia's eyes and she was searching my face, the way she had a habit of doing. Her eyelashes were so long and pretty; all of a sudden I had a terrible vision of them falling out, one by one. It broke my heart and I had to work very hard to convince myself it didn't matter. We would sacrifice her lovely lashes if we had to. It didn't matter; it would be a small price to pay in return for Azaylia's health, and they would grow back, longer and thicker and even more beautiful than they were before.

• • •

'Trick or treat!'

Ashley was wearing a creepy clown outfit and I was dressed in a frilly black and white skeleton dress. The Covid rules were relaxed a little for Halloween and we were allowed to go around the ward, giving out sweets to the other children. We weren't permitted to do it together, unfortunately, but we managed to have a photo taken in the foyer, which was nice. Then we took it in turns to do our bit and invited the other kids to knock on Azaylia's door and shout 'trick or treat?' Azaylia was loving all the activity and fuss, gurgling and smiling and reacting with excitement every time there was another face at the window.

In the afternoon I changed her into a little purple witch's dress with a pointy hat and carried her down the corridor. It was a treat for me just to leave the room with her on my hip and she seemed to love seeing the other children. Some were dressed up in Halloween costumes too, though others were too poorly to climb out of their pyjamas, or their mother's arms.

I hadn't spoken to any of the other parents on Ward 18. We normally only saw each other at the door when we were swapping shifts with our partners and it would be a case of sharing a quick look that said, 'Yeah, I know what you're going through.' We still didn't really speak now. This was a time for us to enjoy seeing kids being kids and to simply smile and laugh together.

'Go on, have another one,' Ashley said, passing around his pumpkin tub stuffed with sweets. 'Have as many as you like!' The children's eyes were alight. I was in awe of every single one of those kids. Most gave no real clue about the pain or discomfort they were in. They smiled and they joined in with as much enthusiasm as they could, just as Azaylia did.

Since day one on this ward, I'd noticed that Azaylia was always ready with a smile for the doctors and nurses. She was blessed with such a naturally sunny personality, that was obvious, but were we always reading her right? In the dead of night, when I was trying and failing to snatch some sleep, scary thoughts would gnaw away at me. *Had the nurses got her pain relief dose right? How could Azaylia tell us if they didn't?* I'd tell myself not to worry. Azaylia would cry and let us know, because that's how babies behaved. Azaylia did grizzle when she wanted something and she had quiet and less responsive moments too. *You could tell when something wasn't quite right, so there was no need to panic, was there?* I tried to listen to this voice of reason in my head, but I didn't always succeed. There were moments when I couldn't stop my mind spiralling back in time. How much pain had Azaylia been in before she was diagnosed? I'd think about the colic drops and the thrush medicine and the laxatives and the nasal spray and feel pangs of guilt and fear. *Was she suffering? Did we miss something? Could we have done more? Why hadn't she been diagnosed sooner? Would that have changed everything?* Once again, I'd force myself to cling to reason. We had kept going back to the doctor, again and again. We were here now and Azaylia was receiving the most amazing care.

Despite what the oncologist had warned might happen, the chemo wasn't taking Azaylia – it was the opposite. She was smashing her way through it, fighting like the warrior Ashley told her she was. The doctors and nurses were amazed at how strong she was. The odds had been stacked against her and they all knew that. They had been prepared for the worst; I'd seen it in the faces of so many members of her medical team. They were the experts and professionals and they would not have been surprised if her little body couldn't cope with the amount of chemo she was being blasted with. But Ashley and me didn't go there: we kept up 100 per cent trust and belief in Azaylia, and she matched our faith with her grit and determination.

Ashley loved playing peek-a-boo with Azaylia, ducking down at the side of her cot and then jumping up to surprise her. When she laughed, her whole face lit up, throwing out sunbeams around the room. We sang 'If You're Happy And You Know It' and she loved that too, giggling when we clapped our hands. The more she engaged with us, the more we encouraged her to do. We taught her to take a tight hold of her rattles, to encourage her motor skills, and she started to reach out and grab at the nurses' masks and pens, pulling them out of their pockets.

'Are you bullying me?' they'd laugh, delighted by her fighting spirit and cheeky personality.

We'd been told Azaylia would not be able to eat, but I tried her on a rusk and she loved it, attempting to stuff the whole thing in her mouth. I started making her baby rice and porridge and giving her yoghurt, and she loved those too.

The nurses were surprised every step of the way, and I was determined to keep surprising them. It was almost as if the more I was told 'she can't', the more I said 'she will'.

We had also been warned that Azaylia wouldn't be able to sit up, because she would be lethargic during her chemo, but she did. We put her in a pink Bumbo seat, which is like a plastic booster chair with cutout sections for the legs, and she sat upright, supported by blankets, with no problem at all.

'Look at you in your Bumbo seat, clever girl!' I said.

She gave me the brightest smile. It must have been so good for Azaylia to sit up like that. She spent so many hours lying in her cot and you could see the excitement on her face as she looked around the room and reached out for the toys we set out all around her.

One of Azaylia's favourite toys was a toy piano that lit up and made sounds. When she was lying down I put it at the bottom of the cot and she loved kicking it to see what happened next.

Matty's girlfriend Amy saw videos of her booting the life out of it. Azaylia was holding her own dummy and grabbing her teddies too, moving them around – 'Anaya's not even doing all those things yet!' Amy said. But we had all day long to sit with Azaylia, to teach her things and to encourage her to improve her strength and hand-to-eye coordination. Why wouldn't we do as much as we possibly could with her?

'When she gets better, she will need all these skills,' I said. 'Why not teach her now?'

Ashley agreed, and we both made sure as much play and learning time as possible was added into her routine every single day. We both loved singing Disney songs to Azaylia. Her favourite was 'I Wanna Be Like You' from *The Jungle Book*. It's such an upbeat song and the vibe of it suited her down to the ground. She wanted to live her best life and she responded to the music every time, jiggling her little legs and batting her arms around excitedly.

A friend had sent in a Nala cuddly toy from *The Lion King* and we'd got her Simba so she had the pair. Azaylia adored them. I'd zoom them around her cot and she tracked them as if she was a little lioness herself, keeping an eye on its prey. Sharp as a tack, she was not letting those cuddly toys out of her sight, not for a single second.

This little champ was going to grow into an amazing little girl, I was sure of that. She was spirited, she was resourceful; she had a huge heart and she would grab life with both hands. I visualised her going to school, in a little uniform. I could see her in a sports kit too, trying to keep up with Ashley, or maybe even playing tennis, just like he hoped she would. Best of all, I imagined her looking poised and self-confident, wearing beautiful clothes and going out to have so much fun, just like I had when I met her daddy. I invited these images in; I welcomed them with open arms and held them tight in my heart. *The law of attraction.* Think it, dream it, and there is so much more chance it will happen. All of this *was* going to happen for my daughter.

· · ·

We'd been on Ward 18 for weeks now and, as well as embracing my role as Miss Positivity, I'd developed a powerful alter ego – Question Girl. Azaylia had to have her stats taken every four hours, so a nurse would come in at regular intervals through the night to check that things like her oxygen level, temperature and blood pressure were where they should be. I'd learned what every machine did, exactly what medication Azaylia was due and when, and I was on high alert, snapping my eyes open every time a nurse arrived. I was like a human version of one of those sensor lights that detect movement and instantly powers up.

My bones would always creak when I uncurled myself from the red chair and I was so sleep-deprived my brain would protest, refusing to flex and sharpen as quickly as I wanted it to. Still, I never let them win. I didn't care how many times I got up and I never counted up how many minutes or hours of sleep I managed to get. Whether it was two, three or four o'clock in the morning, I was awake and keeping watch the second there was any activity in the room. Even if Azaylia stirred ever so quietly, just for a second, I'd hear her and I'd be straight by her side, stroking her head and her hands and telling her, 'Mummy is here.' It was precious time with my daughter, that's how I saw it. I was very lucky to be able to share these moments – it was like a bonus gift.

One night, I woke up to find Azaylia was sound asleep and there was no nurse in the room. It must have been the bad dream I was having that jolted me awake. My head had been invaded with terrifying images of white cars, multiplying fast and furiously. There were hundreds and thousands of white cars and just two red cars. The white cars were big and shiny and the little red cars were hooting their horns, driving round in circles and crashing into walls because they had no way through.

'Boom!' The sound of the collisions ripped through me. That's what woke me up, I realised, and now I was trying to force myself to focus on beautiful things, like Azaylia's soft skin and the pretty lights outside the window. I thought of sunrises and sunsets, rainbows and moonlight. When she was better, I would take Azaylia to see the Northern Lights and all the other wonders of the world. Azaylia was a pure, innocent and very beautiful baby. Good would prevail. She was loved so deeply and the whole world was sharing in that love. You only had to look around the room to see that, let alone go on Instagram. Toys and clothes were arriving daily at the hospital and we had presents stacked up everywhere. We didn't ask for anything but prayers, but strangers kept sending the most thoughtful presents along with their messages of love on social media. It was truly heartwarming.

. . .

'It's the tea trolley,' I said to Azaylia. 'What's Mummy going to have today?'

By the time the tea lady did her rounds we'd already spent hours going through our morning routine. A nurse had been in to give Azaylia her 0.3ml syringe of Oramorph, the milk in the unit that fed her NG tube was replenished and I'd washed and changed Azaylia probably half a dozen times, following a very specific routine. There was a little sick bowl at the end of her bed and I filled it with water, added some Dermawash, washed and dried her bottom using disposable wash cloths called Conti wipes and applied bottom cream. It was a routine the hospital had got us into even before Azaylia started chemo, because her skin was too delicate to use ordinary baby wipes. Azaylia's catheter had been removed by now and you could see the toxic blue medicine seeping into her nappy.

As we'd been taught, I wore gloves when I changed her, to protect my own skin, and I worked as quickly as possible, to protect hers. In between doing all the jobs it was either nap time or playtime and, come what may, I always left the room spick and span, ready for Ashley when he arrived to take over.

I always felt some excitement when I heard the clatter of the tea trolley. The toast was more like soggy bread but I took it gratefully. It was usually cold by the time I ate it, just like the coffee, but that's being a mum for you. I accepted the deal completely. I was a mummy now. I was Azaylia's mummy, and I would be Azaylia's mummy forever.

I told her that, when the hands on the clock nudged towards midday, it was time for me to kiss her goodbye until tomorrow.

'Mummy loves you,' I said. 'Mummy will always love you!'

Ashley was waiting at the hospital entrance, where we always met at the same time every day to swap over.

'She's doing great,' I told him, giving him a smile. 'Enjoy yourselves!'

'We will,' he said.

And I knew that he would, however he was feeling and however hard it might be to get through another day and night on that ward. There was no other way but to keep smiling, just like Azaylia.

CHAPTER
TEN

'You're still so beautiful,' Ashley said, stroking Azaylia's hair. 'You know that? You'll always be the most beautiful girl in the world.'

Her soft baby hair was starting to fall out. You could see wisps on her pillow and thin patches were appearing on her scalp. 'This means your treatment is working,' he added. 'So we don't worry about it, yeah? We embrace it, we accept it. We will get through this, baby.'

This was typical of Ashley, looking for a positive in the most upsetting, heartbreaking situation. We were on FaceTime, as we often were. He told me he'd been dancing with Azaylia that morning, singing Whitney Houston's 'I Wanna Dance With Somebody' to her when she woke at the crack of dawn and he woke half a second later and scooped her in his arms.

After we finished the call, I found myself smiling about the fact Ashley had wanted a boy at first. Look at him now!

When I found out I was having a girl, I'd wondered if she would want to grow her hair really long, just like I did when I was a little girl. It was just one of the many daydreams I had when I knew I was having a daughter. My hair was so long as a kid I could sit on it, and it was my pride and joy.

My parents ran a property letting business together, before they separated. Some of their tenants were down on their luck and they'd come to our door and ask to borrow milk, or a pound. 'I'm not feeling too good,' they'd say. 'Can I have my tablets?' Mum would pick up their prescriptions and look after their medications for them as a way of helping them. *Why do they keep taking these tablets? I always used to think. They're not fixing these people, are they? What's the point in these tablets?*

There was one man who would always try to pat me on the head when he came to the house. I'd never forgotten him, though I would only have been six or seven years old. If my hair was messed up in any way at all it really aggravated me. I hated having even a single hair out of place and I'd duck and run for cover. In the end I used to sit and watch out of the side of our net curtains, so I could run and hide if ever the man who patted my head came to the door.

The memories got me thinking about Azaylia's future and what lay in store for her. Maybe she'd be the opposite of me, preferring to have her hair cropped short and not giving two hoots if it was messed up? She could do anything she wanted to do. She could wear what she liked, do any job she wanted and live anywhere in the world. As long as she was healthy. As long as she was alive and kicking. Nothing else mattered.

• • •

We had another meeting with a specialist and I went over to the hospital to meet Ashley. As we sat and waited for the doctor to arrive we chatted about what else he'd been doing that morning. Singing and dancing were the things Ashley chose to share with me on FaceTime – and with his Instagram followers – but as usual so many other things had happened on the ward. For one thing, Azaylia had been sick all down his front. He was used to cleaning her up, we both were. The sickness was another side effect of her chemo and we had to wear gloves when we dealt with that too and dispose of any clothes she was sick on.

'How's her skin?' I asked. 'Did you use the cream on her bum?'

'Yeah, of course, Safiyya. It's getting better. She heals fast, she's a trouper.'

The further Azaylia had got into her chemo, the redder and sorer her bottom became. It was so bad, it was red raw and she developed a nasty abscess, which really upset us. The nurses explained that it was the chemo burning her skin, because however quick we were to change her nappy, any contact with the skin was damaging. From that moment on we'd started to leave her nappy open and we never took our eyes off her, so we could immediately see if she needed to be changed. As soon as the tiniest amount of blue urine appeared, we'd whip the old nappy away, clean Azaylia with Conti wipes and lay a fresh nappy underneath her so there was the very least possible contact between the skin and the chemo. We were changing her half a dozen times an hour; sometimes more, and we were also using a product called Medihoney to heal her skin.

'Why didn't anybody tell us to do this in the first place?' I said. 'This need not have happened!'

As well as being Question Girl, I'd become super protective and hyper-vigilant over my daughter. I was watching the nurses like a hawk too, double-checking everything they did. Sometimes when one nurse left the room I'd have the same conversation with the next one. I wanted to make absolutely sure nothing had been missed and I also wanted to be sure that I understood everything that was happening to my daughter. Education was empowering me, because the more I knew, the more use I felt I could be to Azaylia.

Ashley was the voice of reason, gently reminding me that the priority for the nurses was to give Azaylia the medication she needed and to, quite literally, nurse her. They weren't there to teach people like us how to parent a child with cancer. They did their level best, but they simply didn't have the time to monitor everything we did. We had to trust the nurses to do their job – and they *were* doing a brilliant job – and it was up to us to support them as best we could and to do our best to learn how to be cancer parents as we went along.

Azaylia had surprised everyone by coping with the chemo so well and this meeting was about what would happen next. She was to have a second round of chemo, we'd been told. The first round had knocked her leukaemia count right down to zero and I assumed the purpose of this second round was to kill off any cells that might have been missed. I took it as a good sign. After all, we'd been warned that Azaylia might not survive one round of chemo, but she'd taken it like a champ and now they were giving her a second. She must be doing so well.

Once again, I asked the specialist if I could record the meeting and I'm so glad I did. The doctor took her time, patiently explaining all the results of Azaylia's treatment so far, and then she discussed the details of the next round of chemotherapy. I was very calm and attentive, taking it all in, but then she said something I was totally unprepared for: Azaylia was going to need a bone marrow transplant.

'What? Why?'

I felt totally blindsided and my heart raced in my chest. Suddenly I was hearing that Azaylia's cancer was so aggressive chemo alone would not save her. It was like having a gun fired at my kneecaps and I felt paralysed in my chair. I looked at Ashley in horror, searching his face for answers, but he looked as frightened and stunned as I was.

I had no understanding of what a bone marrow transplant was and my mind was going haywire. I started asking questions but the doctor's answers weren't making sense to me. It was as if her words had been scrambled up and tipped into my head. My brain was spinning like a tombola, throwing alien, random words at me. They landed like lucky dip booby prizes and I had no idea what to do with them. Meanwhile, my heart had solidified in my chest: we'd gone back to square one in the blink of an eye.

We knew nothing about bone marrow transplants and we were both listening very carefully to the doctor and taking in everything she said: Azaylia would need a donor and we'd need to find a match.

Ashley had gone very quiet and it was me who asked the crucial question: 'How easy will it be to find a bone marrow donor for Azaylia?'

The doctor hesitated momentarily, which terrified me. This was clearly not an easy question to answer.

Both our mums are white-British, Ashley's paternal grandparents came to the UK from St Vincent in the Caribbean and I can trace my ancestors to Burma and India. The doctor had to be honest with us. They would search the donor registers, but Azaylia's mixed Caribbean, Burmese, Indian and English ethnicity could make it very difficult to find a match.

Ashley looked weak and lost, but he still managed to come out with some fighting talk: 'We'll find one,' he said. 'We'll fight as hard as Azaylia is fighting and we'll find one.'

When we stepped out of that room I was floating down the corridor again, like I had when I first arrived on Ward 18. My body was not my own. I was somewhere else entirely, trying to process the shock of this setback.

The doctors had never promised us that the chemo would cure Azaylia, but I'd clung to that hope, especially when she dealt with it so amazingly well. I could see now I'd been living one day at a time, celebrating small victories and keeping hope alive always. I made a point of trying to be in the moment with Azaylia, believing in her, living by the rules of Club 100 and refusing to let negativity come anywhere near her.

It was November 2020 now and we'd been in hospital for a month. Christmas was the only place in the future I'd been allowing my brain to go. I'd been dreaming of us all being at home, this nightmare finally behind us by then. The chemo would have blasted all of Azaylia's cancer away by then, my little girl would be in remission and we'd have the biggest celebration ever.

I remembered last Christmas well.

'Here's your card,' we'd said casually to our parents, when we saw them on Christmas Eve. We'd put our eight-week scan picture in Christmas cards for Ashley's mum, his dad and my mum and stepdad, and then we stood back and watched for their reactions. They were completely taken aback but the room was instantly full of oohs and ahhs, all their eyes alight with happiness. They hadn't seen this coming. We were still kids to them, going out and having fun, with no responsibilities. But they could not have been happier for us and each one of them cried with joy.

On Christmas Day itself we had waited until all the other members of Ashley's side of the family were in the pub together, including all the aunties and uncles, grandparents and cousins. 'We're having a baby!' we announced, watching more smiles appear and more tears roll. We did the same with my side of the family, going round to my auntie's house to tell my aunts and cousins and uncles, all at the same time.

I can remember that I'd had a little daydream about having our baby at the table for Christmas dinner the following year. *This year.* The magic experience of Christmas that I'd had myself as a child was going to come back. It was a thrilling thought. My nephew Noah would be able to play with his new cousin and I would be with my brother, doing so many fun things. We'd go to see the Christmas lights switched on and we could visit the grotto to see Santa.

Am I going to be OK at being a mum? That was something else on my mind, at that early stage in my pregnancy. I can remember looking around at all our relatives and thinking, *How will I learn how to do everything? How do you go to the shops with a baby? Do you have to carry the car seat in with you, or what?*

Looking back, it was like watching a stranger, or an unsuspecting character in a film who has no idea of the nightmare they are about to step into.

• • •

My priority now was to learn everything I could about bone marrow and, as Ashley headed back to the hotel and I went to the ward, I told him to do whatever he felt was right in terms of sharing this setback on social media. I could already see his mind ticking over. We had to find a donor and maybe social media could help? As desperate as it might be, we were both thinking the same thing. Maybe one of our followers could help? What did we have to lose?

When I walked into her room, Azaylia was smiling and giggling. There was one particular nurse she really took to and we always tried to get her to step into the room when both Ashley and me were in a meeting. The nurse was encouraging Azaylia to play with 'Smooth Moves Sloth', one of her favourite toys who danced and sang songs and had a belly that lit up. Sloth was designed for kids of nine months plus, but Azaylia was already learning how to press his buttons if she wanted music and lights.

'Go, Azaylia!' I said, delighted to see her so interested and alert. 'You've got this!'

Azaylia gave me the brightest smile I'd ever seen. It instantly lifted me, which was hardly surprising – it could have lit up the whole hospital. My heart overflowed with love for her. She was so incredibly ill, yet she was giving out so much love and her strength was radiating out of her small body. I felt Azaylia's power charge through me, replenishing some of the optimism that had fallen away in the meeting with the doctor.

'We'll find you a donor, princess,' I said. 'Don't you worry. We'll get you that transplant and then we'll be out of here, won't we?'

My voice was quivering, I realised. I wanted to be as optimistic as I had been before, but it wasn't easy. I was struggling to keep myself together, but I had to – if Azaylia could smile, there was no way I was crumbling.

'Right,' I said. 'What are we going to play with now?'

I handed her one of her favourite dollies. Emily wore a pink hat and, for some reason, Azaylia liked to hit her in the face. Sure enough, she punched Emily right on the nose.

'You're such a cheeky girl,' I said, bursting out laughing.

• • •

While Azaylia was still in her first round of chemo the oncologist who'd told me about the white cars and the red cars came to see me. I told her how much that explanation had helped me and I asked what she could tell me about bone marrow – 'I don't even know what it is,' I said, 'let alone what it does in the body.'

There had been moments when I wondered if the doctors and nurses looked at me and thought I was stupid. I worried about taking up too much of their time, which is why I often asked the same question of several different nurses or members of the medical team. It wasn't like that with this oncologist. She was very patient and understanding, and I knew I could ask her anything and get a jargon-free answer that would really help.

She told me the bone marrow is tissue that fills the inside of your bones and it's like the body's factory because it makes stem cells. The stem cells produce most of the body's essential red and white blood cells as well as platelets, which are colourless blood cells that help blood clot. But in Azaylia's case, there was something going wrong in the factory. It wasn't doing its job properly and she needed a bone marrow transplant to make the factory work correctly. It was a bit like having a new head gasket put in your car: before you replaced the gasket you cleaned the whole engine out, and that's what the chemo was being used for. It was like surgical spirit, wiping away all the contamination the old factory had created. The first round of chemo had worked really well, but that didn't mean the factory itself was fixed. In Azaylia's case, it would only get mended with a transplant. This could be in the form of a bone marrow transplant or a stem cell transplant using blood from another baby's umbilical cord. It was all very complicated, but it was explained to me very well. The stem cells in the umbilical cord are responsible for producing all the blood in the body, I was taught, and can therefore be used as an alternative to bone marrow for transplants.

It was a race against time to find a donor. The doctors didn't use that language, but we understood where we were. However well Azaylia's little body coped with the chemo, and however many more rounds she had, chemo alone was not going to cure her. I had an awful image in my mind. I could see blue chemicals and black cancer cells fighting each other inside Azaylia's body. The leukaemia cells were refusing to lie down and die. The image burned for less than a second on my mind before I pushed it aside, forcing a new picture to appear. I visualised the shiny new head gasket arriving. Azaylia was being given healthy cells and healing blood. I could see the new blood pumping around her body, healing and regenerating her. The white cars had dispersed and the red cars were riding around happily, tooting their horns with joy. They put bright pink roses in her cheeks and filled her lungs with fresh energy. I held that thought and then I imagined myself lifting Azaylia out of her hospital cot one last time. She had no central line, no NG tube. She didn't have any tabs and tubes attached to her at all and I didn't have to put her back in. We were going to walk out of the hospital entrance and go home, to finally start again. That was the image I needed to keep close, and the one I had to believe would become real, one day very soon.

●　●　●

Ashley and me were both on a mission now. We had been talking to the Anthony Nolan Trust, the charity that recruits stem cell donors and helps match them to people with blood cancers like leukaemia. They were already searching through their database for a match, which was fantastic. At the same time, we were educating ourselves. We learned that Azaylia's mixed ethnicity meant she had only a 20 per cent chance of finding a match, compared to 69 per cent for people with white, European heritage.

We began an appeal through our social media to get as many people as possible to sign up to the donor register, and we prepared to put out an appeal through Anthony Nolan for more stem cell donors to come forward. We were also appealing for more blood donors in general, because the blood transfusions Azaylia had in intensive care could not have happened if people didn't donate blood. It had been an eye-opener to us and we'd both vowed to do whatever we could to improve awareness and boost donations to blood banks. It was one small way of paying back the NHS, we had thought, not imagining how long Azaylia would be in hospital and the amount of treatment she would need.

The number of Instagram followers we both had had been growing and growing since we started sharing Azaylia's story. I'd gone from around 4,000 followers to nearly a million, while Ashley was heading to 1.5 million. He also had a huge following on Twitter. We would share the appeal on every platform possible, as well as giving interviews to the press.

Social media can be such a cruel and cynical place and I was aware we'd come in for criticism online for posting up videos and pictures of Azaylia from her hospital bed. Some people had asked why we were wasting time, sharing our story online when we had a sick child to look after, and they had made personal criticisms. I didn't read them. Who cared what anonymous trolls and keyboard warriors said? I wasn't letting any negativity in and I wasn't changing my behaviour for anyone. The response we had on social media was overwhelmingly positive, that's what I focused on. And thank God I did, because now our followers could potentially help save Azaylia's life.

We wrote out our appeal for Anthony Nolan together. 'Our daughter was very poorly when we first arrived in hospital and we knew her chances were very low,' it said. 'But she has done so well with the treatment. She's been amazing but now she needs a stem cell donor. She's learning how to smile, babble and grip on to things. All these milestones that babies reach, but she's doing it all in hospital. She's always smiling, she's a joy to be around every day.'

We felt we'd summed Azaylia up to a tee – she really was a joy to be with.

'When she was first diagnosed I felt like I was dreaming,' the appeal went on, 'life didn't seem real, just knowing that your child could potentially lose their life before your own can't be described, but the only thing we can do to help our daughter is be as positive as possible. That's the only thing we can do. It's out of Azaylia's hands now, she's almost climbed this mountain, but she now needs someone else's hand to help her get to the top. She can't do this on her own, she needs a donor.'

We would also tell our followers how easy it is to join the Anthony Nolan register: You fill in an online form and medical questionnaire, and if you're approved, the charity sends you a swab kit that you complete and post back so they can find out your tissue type. The charity was delighted we were using our platforms to increase awareness and they put out a statement saying that every single person who signed had the potential to give hope to someone like Azaylia.

I was soaking up information at a rate of knots. The Anthony Nolan Trust recruits people aged 16–30 to their register, as research shows younger people are more likely to be chosen to donate. Young men provide more than half of all stem cell donations, but only make up 18 per cent of their register, so Anthony Nolan was particularly calling on men aged 16–30 and those from ethnic minority backgrounds.

Another charity, DKMS, recruits people aged 31–55, and we also contacted them so they could share the appeal. Their response was phenomenal too – we had two amazing charities supporting us and Azaylia's appeal had the potential to save many more lives on top of her own. The two charities combined typically get 30–40,000 people per year registering to be donors and Anthony Nolan typically had about 100 people signing up a day – 'If they get just 100 more people to sign up, there is more hope,' Ashley said.

Hope was all we had, but we had plenty of it. This was going to work – it had to.

CHAPTER
ELEVEN

Ashley FaceTimed me and as soon as I saw his face I knew he had some good news because he was grinning from ear to ear.

'Have we got a donor?' was my initial reaction, but I knew it was too soon as we had only put out the appeal 48 hours before. 'What's going on?' I asked. 'What is it?'

'Babe, you know I said they normally get 30–40,000 people signing up to the register every year.'

'Yeah, go on.'

'Well, Anthony Nolan had 42,000 applicants sign up over the weekend! Normally they'd have 200 in two days. It's the biggest response they've ever had.'

I felt adrenaline shoot all round my body as I took the numbers in. Ashley had said he would be happy if just 100 more people signed up, but 42,000 had signed to one charity alone, in just two days! It was staggering.

I turned my phone round so Ashley could see Azaylia and we both told her the news.

'Let's go, champ!' we cheered excitedly. 'See how many people are helping you, Azaylia! See how much everyone is supporting you!'

I felt so full of pride for Azaylia. Thanks to social media, other people could see the joy she gave us every day. 'It's your beautiful smile that's done this,' I told her. 'This is all down to you, little lady! Yes, it is, clever girl!'

Azaylia was in her second round of chemo now and it was taking its toll. She was sleepier than before and starting to look quite pale and poorly. More of her hair rubbed away on her cot sheets and her pretty eyebrows were looking a little bit thinner. Heartbreakingly, her smiles were harder to find too, which was the hardest thing of all.

'It's playtime!' I told her one morning, trying to keep up the same routine we always had, once she'd had her medication and all the jobs were done. As well as giving Azaylia frequent baths and changing her nappy multiple times every hour, we had to be hyper-cautious about keeping the whole room clean and sterile. Nothing could touch her that hadn't been wiped with a Clinell sterilising wipe. The chemo was stripping away her immunity and to avoid any risk of infection we were sterilising toys, dummies and surfaces non-stop, all the time. It was stressful, not least because I became obsessive and pedantic about it, but I was taking no chances.

'What shall we play with today?' I smiled at Azaylia.

The toy piano was at the end of her bed but she was too lethargic to kick the keys like she normally did so I sat her Sloth toy beside her, but she just stared at it. I could see she was interested and was thinking about reaching out to play with him, and I encouraged her to press one of his buttons, but instead she turned and gave me a look that said she just didn't have it in her today.

We'd been told to expect Azaylia to suffer more this time round, because of the type of chemo she was having and the cumulative effect of it being round two, but I didn't think it would be like this. Round one had lulled us into a false sense of security, I guess. I wanted to believe she would breeze through this one as easily as she did first time round, and me and Ashley had been telling each other as much.

'She's smashed everything!' we said. 'Every time Azaylia is told she can't, she does! She'll sail through this, just wait and see!'

It wasn't the case. In the night Azaylia was awake every couple of hours, grizzling, crying and wriggling around, as if she was in discomfort. My head would be aching from lack of sleep, but I was up with her every single time, trying to soothe her in any way I could. I sang lullabies and our favourite song, Whitney's 'When You Believe'. I stroked her head and hands, and I whispered to her that I loved her and I was there for her. Sometimes I got scared she was in too much pain and I'd call the nurses to check her over and make sure all her mediation had been given correctly, even though I'd watched another nurse do everything earlier and I knew there was nothing more they could give her.

I had to keep telling myself over and over again that the chemo was a necessary evil, essential to her recovery. The goal was to have her cancer markers down to zero – in other words, for her to be leukaemia-free – by the time she had the bone marrow transplant. That way she'd have the best chance of a full recovery when the new 'head gasket' went into her body and started creating healthy blood cells.

Deep down, I was terrified we wouldn't find a match, in spite of the huge response to the appeal. But I trampled on my negative thoughts and stayed as upbeat as I possibly could, even when I was talking to my brother – 'We'll find someone,' I said to Danny. 'We only need one person and more than 40,000 have signed up already. More people are signing up every day.' We knew Azaylia would need more chemo as well as the transplant. 'Then she'll be as good as new, good to go,' I said.

Danny and other close family members were very good at listening to me and they helped me manage my expectations too. They would gently remind me that it would take time for all the potential new donors to be processed and checked for a match, and that, despite the fact that so many people had signed up, Azaylia's mixed ethnicity still made the search difficult. It could take longer to find a match than we wanted it to and I had to be prepared for that.

I knew all this, but it had become second nature for me to be optimistic, or at least to put on my best act around others. When I was on my own in the hotel, my fears would surface. The moment I opened my eyes the frightening questions started.

What if this chemo doesn't work? What if we don't find a match? Will my baby still be here at Christmas?

I'd get in the shower and will myself to trample away these thoughts straight away. I had to empty my mind and wash all these negative thoughts and feelings down the plughole. They were not helpful and I needed to sort myself out and get back to the hospital with my best smile on my face.

I never let Ashley hear my blackest thoughts. Neither of us wanted to give them oxygen. We were offered counselling on a weekly basis in the hospital, but I always passed it up. Why would I want to take time away from Azaylia to focus on myself? I had a set number of minutes and hours in every day to spend with my daughter and I wanted to spend every moment with her. Ashley was the same; he told me he felt like he'd spent years and years with her already, though she was still only four months old. In a way, Covid has helped us, giving us both the gift of so much one-to-one time with Azaylia.

'When we get out of here, we'll have the strongest bond ever with our baby,' I said. 'It will be totally unbreakable, forever.'

. . .

More and more gifts were arriving at the hospital daily, many of them from our social media followers. I was posting updates regularly. These people had started out as strangers, but as they shared our journey I came to see them as friends and family. They had become a big and important part of my community and I was so grateful to them. As well as thoughtful presents and

143

beautiful clothes they were sending in loving messages, poems, and drawings their kids had done for Azaylia. They told us they watched our videos on Instagram and tried to work out what we might need and what we didn't have. It was incredible and their kindness lifted me up on a daily basis. Azaylia was amassing every new sensory toy and baby gadget on the market and our followers were often several steps ahead of us, sending in things like teething rings before she had even started teething. It was so thoughtful and touching. The clothes in particular were a godsend during chemo, as so many vests and babygros had to go straight in the bin after one wear, if Azaylia so much as dribbled on them.

With Christmas approaching, the gifts increased. Bag-loads were delivered every day to the ward and I was sharing out whatever I could with other children in the hospital. Only brand-new items and unopened toys could be donated to other wards and everything had to be sanitised, but it was a pleasure to be able to spread the love and tell our followers that every item was gratefully received and appreciated.

Another parent on Ward 18 stopped Ashley at the door one day. 'I want to thank you,' she said softly.

'What for?' he asked, taken aback.

'You and your partner have changed the way I behave around my little boy. Thank you.'

It was such an amazing compliment and Ashley was very touched by it. The mum told him it started at Halloween, when we dressed up and went round the ward, giving out treats. 'Your positivity has really inspired me,' she said. 'I see you both smiling when you play with your daughter. I see you dancing with her and singing to her, and dressing her up in lovely clothes. Why be any other way?'

I knew there were people out there who questioned how we could even think about things as trivial as Halloween and pretty outfits when our daughter was so ill, or why we would bother spending time sharing our story online. But we would only post a total of three or four minutes a day on a story, and besides, it was all about being positive and staying as upbeat as we could. That big-hearted mother had summed it up: why be any other way?

With the help of the family I ordered in loads of Christmas decorations, determined to make Azaylia's room as fun and festive as possible. Her cousin Noah had already made her a Christmas card and that took pride of place on the wall. We might not be able to sit her in a high chair around the dinner table with our families, but we both agreed that we would pull out all the stops to make her first Christmas as special as we could.

'When she's older, I want her to look back and see that we made the biggest effort for her when she was in hospital,' I'd said to my brother. He'd been up to the hotel to deliver some home-cooked food, which he did all the time, despite the fact he was working two jobs and wouldn't get back to Nuneaton until 10pm at night. Danny gave me the proudest big-brother smile ever. His encouragement meant so much – we'd become closer than ever in recent months and he above everyone knew how much it meant to me to give my daughter the best childhood memories possible.

'I want her to know how much we cared,' I said, 'and how much we tried to bring her as much happiness as possible.'

I was echoing what I'd said when Azaylia was a newborn and I first started to share pictures and videos online, but now there was even more reason to create memories. When Azaylia was big enough to take part in the school Nativity, or write out her own Christmas list to send to Santa, we could sit around the tree together, look back at all the photos and videos and she would see that Christmas wasn't cancelled, even though she was in hospital

'Look,' I'd tell her. 'Even though you were so poorly, we celebrated with you, Azaylia. We all had a very special time together, and lots of fun in hospital.'

. . .

Azaylia was still struggling through the second round of chemo and was looking pale and sickly. Her eyes were quite puffy, which was upsetting to see. Every time I looked at her, I couldn't help wondering what else might be happening inside her little body. Was the chemo working fast enough? *Of course it was*, I told myself. *It's doing its job. She's gonna breeze through this, just like we said she would. She'll be in good shape in time for her transplant.*

We knew Azaylia's next round of chemo would be stronger and more potent than before. She would be left infertile, we had been warned, because of the strength of this particular chemo. It was so shocking to hear that. It was something we'd have to talk about with her when she was old enough, I thought. It would be incredibly tough, but if that's what she had to give up in order to survive, of course we had to accept it. Azaylia would have to accept it too one day. The thought was devastating.

Enough time had passed by now for potential donors to start being identified and we were desperately hoping for news every day. When it finally came, I expected it to be a big, dramatic moment, but it wasn't like that at all. Ashley and me were in the hotel together, talking to the head of the transplant team on Zoom, because she was isolating at home.

She was helping prepare us for what to expect when Azaylia had the transplant and during the course of our conversation she mentioned that they had two possible matches – one from an umbilical cord and the other from an adult donor. The relief that swept through my body was so powerful, it was incredible. There were lots of steps that had to be taken and we'd get more information soon, we were told. There were no guarantees yet, but fundamentally it was good news.

I had so many questions to ask, but I would be patient. All of this had happened in a matter of weeks and we'd have to sit tight and wait for further tests to take place.

'We knew it, didn't we?' I said to Ashley when the call was over. 'It was always going to happen. It's the power of Azaylia, it's what she deserves!'

Though I was matching Ashley in his positive talking, in truth I'd been terrified of not finding a donor. Of course I had, and this felt like an absolute miracle, sent from above. Still, it was very early days and there were lots of hurdles to jump first.

We kept the news to ourselves, sharing it with only a few close family members.

Further down the line we found out that the preferred donor was a baby. If all went to plan, Azaylia would receive stem cells from its umbilical cord. This was preferable to the adult donor, because the cells were brand new. However, it meant the donor would always remain anonymous, because the cord belongs to the baby, not the mother, and a baby could not give consent. I remember thinking that was a pity because one day in the future it would have been nice for Azaylia to meet the person who saved her life.

I had no idea how the stem cells were collected or transplanted in Azaylia, let alone how they could repair her faulty bone marrow. Once again, there was so much to learn and I had a million questions to ask.

Over the next few days and weeks we spoke to a specialist who talked us through exactly how the stem cells are collected from the donor and given to Azaylia and we had more Zoom meetings with the head of stem cell transplants. I was hungry for all the information I could get and I was very grateful to both for all the time they spent with us.

When I first heard that Azaylia needed a transplant I imagined something would have to come out of her body before the transplant went in, and therefore she would need surgery of some kind. But this wasn't anything like an organ transplant. To help me understand, I was told to imagine the umbilical cord is basically like a sausage with blood in it. They extract the blood soon after the birth, flattening the cord and pulling the blood out with a syringe before freezing it at -190 degrees C. On the day of the transplant, the defrosted blood is delivered through a tube, into a vein, just like in a blood transfusion. Azaylia's donated blood would be syringed in slowly, through her central line, and Ashley and me would be able to take turns to sit with her while the transfusion took place.

All of this was a relief to hear. We would each be able to hold her hand in turn and offer reassurances, and that was such a comfort.

'What happens next?' I asked, nervously.

We were clearly only a fraction of the way through the explanation and I was digging my fingernails into the palms of my hands and gritting my teeth, waiting to hear more. Ashley had determination etched in every line on his face. He looked exhausted, but he was alert and focused all the way through.

'We have to wait for it to engraft,' we were told.

'What does that mean?' We asked the same question in unison, which somehow managed to make us both smile. It was a moment that showed us just how tightly we were bound together in this fight. Ever since Ashley declared that Azaylia's room was Club 100, we hadn't had a single discussion about how we would behave or what we would do to get through the next stage, and the next. We were on the same page, every step of the way. Each of us had knuckled down, doing whatever we could to help support Azaylia. Ashley was as quizzical as me and we were a team now: we were Azaylia's mummy and daddy, partners joined in a mission to save our little girl.

It was explained to us that 'engraftment' is a process in which the transplanted stem cells travel through the blood to the bone marrow. When the new cells start to grow and make healthy white and red blood cells and platelets, then your body is accepting them, or 'engrafting'. Engraftment can take weeks or months. One transplant patient in Birmingham needed a full year for the process to complete, we were told, and if you got to 100 per cent engraftment that's a huge milestone in your recovery.

'Not every patient reaches 100 per cent engraftment,' the specialist cautioned, which sparked a passionate outburst from me.

'Azaylia will do it,' I said defiantly. 'She'll give you 100 per cent, I guarantee it. She's hit so many milestones already, ones we were told she never would. She sailed through her first chemo, she's getting through this one. She's so strong, she *wants* to live. Trust me, I know my daughter will give you 100 per cent.'

Ashley agreed completely. 'We know our daughter, she's a fighter. Azaylia will give you 100 per cent.'

The doctors were always very kind and compassionate, allowing us our moments of positive talk, but they had to manage our expectations too and inform us about all the other potential outcomes.

We'd been down this road before and I braced myself. We were told we could have lost Azaylia to the first round of chemotherapy, but we didn't. Whatever I was about to hear were worst-case scenarios, ones that were not going to happen to my little girl.

Once again, there was no dressing this up. It was possible we could lose Azaylia during the transplant. Her body might shut down and she could have organ failure. We had to be prepared for that. If she survived the transplant, she could get a host of different diseases. She would be so susceptible to infections she would have to stay in a specially sealed room, where everything was sterile, even the air. Ashley and me would have to follow extremely strict rules about entering the room and she could be in there for three months, six months or even a year – it was impossible to predict.

I'm not sure how I stayed upright in my seat, but I did. I was aching from the inside and my cheeks had gone numb as I tried to process this.

The doctor started to explain how painstaking the routine needed to be, whenever we entered her area on Ward 19, where she would be moved to for the transplant. There was a suction vent system in operation. You entered an anteroom first and, as soon as you stepped in the door, Azaylia's area was automatically air-locked to keep out any pollution or particles we might have brought in from outside. We would have to provide four sets of clothes each that would be washed at 60 degrees C, tumble-dried and put into sealed bags. They would never leave the hospital. We'd have to shower and change into the clean clothes before we went through to Azaylia's room and everything we touched would have to be Clinell-wiped.

I didn't care what Ashley and me had to do. By this point I was sitting there nodding and not questioning a thing. They could have told me I had to bathe in disinfectant five times a day and I'd have agreed to it. We were stepping into an alien world, but it would be a walk in the park for us, compared to what Azaylia would be going through.

CHAPTER
TWELVE

'How is she?' I asked.

'Safiyya, you should have seen her,' Ashley laughed, puffing out white clouds into the freezing December air. We were swapping over outside the hospital as usual and Ashley was dressed in shorts and a thin T-shirt. He didn't seem to notice, or care, how cold it was. Both of us had tunnel vision. Our personal needs had been forgotten. We were completely focused on Azaylia's every move, watching and monitoring her like hawks and giving her all our energy and attention. Azaylia needed to complete this round of chemo, get past Christmas and the New Year and then she would have her transplant in January 2021.

Despite the fact we were always phoning and messaging each other, I was always desperate to hear the latest update from Ashley when I saw him face to face.

'What's she been up to?' I smiled, because Ashley's laughter has always been infectious.

'She's been playing with Simba,' he grinned. 'She was literally rolling, wrestling and growling at that little lion for hours. She's such a fighter! Her energy levels are second to none.'

Ashley had filmed Azaylia playing and when I saw the video my heart melted. She looked as pure and beautiful as she always did, but she also looked so much stronger than she had when I left her the day before. She was lying on her back with Simba on her chest and her arms lifted in a fighting pose.

'Her mittens look like little white boxing gloves,' I giggled. 'That's my girl! What a champ!'

It was my turn with Azaylia now. Ashley had put up a Christmas tree and I was tying stockings to the headboard of her cot. As long as decorations were brand new and sealed in their packages, we were allowed to bring them into Azaylia's room, and they didn't need sterilising unless she was going to touch them. It was the same with gifts and any other items we brought in, but as soon as Azaylia was going to be in contact with something, I was all over it, giving it a thorough wipe-over with the Clinell sterilising wipes.

'What's Mummy doing, Azaylia?' I said, talking to her constantly as I made the room look pretty. 'Look, there's a stocking for Mummy with a snowman on, one for Daddy with a Christmas tree and one for Azaylia. Can you see what's on yours? It's a reindeer!'

I was doing my best to make things feel as Christmassy as possible, but it was harder than ever to stay upbeat. It wasn't meant to be like this. We should be at home, hanging a stocking in Azaylia's bedroom and putting a 'Santa stop here!' sign outside our front door.

Ashley was struggling too. I could see it in his eyes, even when he laughed and on the happy, smiley videos he made with Azaylia. But he was still managing to stay positive.

'Christmas is my favourite day of the year,' he wrote on Instagram, 'and usually I would be spending it seeing my huge family from both my mom and my dad's side. Going to the pub, visiting everyone's houses, having a drink, stuffing my face with an amazing Christmas dinner and spending an amazing day with all my amazing family with everyone in the most amazing spirit. This year however, I will be seeing none of these people and will be doing none of these things. I will be spending it in hospital. But there is no place I'd rather be because it'll be the first Christmas with my AMAZING daughter who changed my life, saved my life and enhanced my life more than I could ever wish to imagine!

'CHRISTMAS IS STILL MY FAVOURITE DAY OF THE YEAR BECAUSE I'M SPENDING IT WITH YOU! #LetsGoChamp'

Reading Ashley's posts always gave me a boost, helping me to re-focus, look for positives and keep my Club 100 promise.

As it had worked out, it would be my turn to wake up Azaylia on Christmas morning. I was very lucky indeed to get to spend that precious time with her and I reminded myself of that. And the most important thing of all was that Azaylia was still fighting. She had everything going for her and, before we knew it, she'd have the transplant and be on the road to a full recovery.

I had to believe that, and I *did* believe it. I had to keep looking for positives and bringing good energy into the room, it was the only way.

I dressed up Azaylia in a gorgeous white vest with a frilly white skirt and matching booties and headband and she looked as pretty as a picture. On her little white vest it said 'Azaylia's 1st Christmas' in sparkly red letters and she had a new red blanket embroidered with golden stars – 'Azaylia Diamond Cain' it said. 'My first Christmas. Let's Go Champ!'

Azaylia Diamond Cain … I stared at her beautiful name and smiled, letting my mind wander back in time.

• • •

'Azaylia,' I was saying to Ashley, holding my mobile with one hand and rubbing my bump with the other. 'What do you think of the name Azaylia?'

He was in Asda, picking up something for dinner, along with my regular order of strawberry Yazoos.

'Azaylia? Yeah, yeah …'

'It's very different and I think I really like it, Ash, but I'm not totally sure. I keep having to say it to myself, but something's sticking …'

A friend had put me onto a baby names website but nothing had appealed to me until now, despite spending hours searching through list after list. I wanted something unusual, like my own name. I've never met another Safiyya and I wanted the same for my daughter, so that as soon as you said her name everyone knew exactly who she was.

'It's unusual,' I went on. 'What do you think?'

'Yeah, babe, er, what was that last thing you said?'

It was a bad line and I could hear the noise of the checkout. 'We'll talk about it later!' I said.

In the event we didn't return to the conversation until the next day, when Ashley brought it up again.

'Safiyya, I've got the name Azaylia in my notes,' he said. 'I really like it – what d'you think?'

'Of course I like it,' I said. 'I rang you with it yesterday, remember? When you were shopping?'

'What?'

'In Asda?'

He looked at me blankly. Ashley was convinced he'd come up with the name all by himself. It didn't matter – we both liked it, and the more we said it, the more we started to love it. We kept sleeping on it though; this was a major decision and we both had to be 100 per cent sure.

'Azaylia Lion Cain,' Ashley declared out of the blue, a few days later. 'That's it!'

I hadn't got as far as a middle name, but it certainly wasn't going to be this.

'Lion? No, Ashley! Can you imagine when she's older? She'll be a beautiful girl and she'll have to say "my name is Azaylia Lion Cain". It's not happening!'

He wasn't giving in easily and, when I wouldn't budge, he tried to get his mum and his sister on board to help his case – 'She's going to be born in August and she'll be a Leo too,' he said. 'Lion is perfect.'

He got their votes, but I still wasn't having it.

'I don't care what you say, she is not going to be Azaylia Lion!' I said, and I swiftly started searching for better ideas.

I discovered that Ashley's grandma's side of the family in St Vincent were all Diamonds. How cool was that?

'What about Diamond? She'll be pretty, she'll dazzle. Azaylia Diamond Cain will shine like a jewel! And how lovely to keep the name going in the family!'

Ashley agreed 100 per cent, thank God. Everybody loved it and I was so happy my daughter would have a name she would be proud to say out loud.

The memory put a smile on my face. I leaned into her cot and told her she was prettier than all the diamonds in the world.

'Azaylia Diamond Cain, I love you to the moon and back, and all round every star in the sky and the whole universe! And guess what? You're a little lion anyway!'

. . .

Christmas presents kept arriving, from friends and family and well-wishers all over the country. The love and support were always appreciated and every time another package arrived, it warmed my heart – 'Look, Azaylia,' I'd say. 'Everyone loves you! Everyone can see what a special girl you are!' People had been so kind, though the gifts sometimes brought me mixed feelings. Deep inside, feelings of despair would be trying to surface. No amount of thoughtfulness or generosity could give Azaylia the gift she needed. I always pushed thoughts like that away, but they would never quite disappear.

Ashley and me hadn't even talked about what to get Azaylia for Christmas. She wanted for nothing in terms of material goods and she already had the most important gift from us – our undivided care, love, attention, time and devotion. I wanted to do something special, though, and one night, when I was on my own in hospital, I decided I wanted to open a bank account for our daughter. It was an investment in her future, I thought.

I called Danny and asked his advice about which account to open, and then I sat on my chair next to Azaylia's bed, opened up my laptop and started to fill in the online application form. All the while I made a point about thinking nothing but positive thoughts. If the law of attraction worked the way I willed it to, this money would attract the riches of good health and a successful life, abundant in love and good fortune.

I decided to deposit £500, but the amount was irrelevant. It didn't matter how much money I put in Azaylia's bank account. This was a symbolic investment in Azaylia herself, and in the future she deserved.

•   •   •

On Christmas Day, it was very emotional waking up in hospital, watching and waiting for the moment Azaylia opened her eyes.

'Happy Christmas, princess,' I whispered as she turned her pretty face towards me. 'Shall we see if Santa has been?'

She fixed her big blue eyes on me and they twinkled brighter than all the baubles and lights decked around the room. I was incredibly grateful to be here, but at the same time I felt so sorry that Ashley wasn't with us to share this special moment.

The Covid rules were relaxed for one day only, so we would be allowed to spend two hours together later in the day. It was a bonus, but it was also very frustrating. 'We're in the most tragic situation of our lives,' I'd said when I found out. 'If we're allowed to be together on Christmas Day, why can't we spend a couple of hours together every day? What difference does it make, just because Santa is coming? Surely it's safe or it isn't?'

I quickly had a word with myself. *What would Azaylia say? What would Azaylia think?* I knew the answers straight away. She would say thank you. She would be grateful for *anything*, and she would be right. Stay positive. Enjoy what you have instead of lamenting what you can't have. That's what I told myself, very firmly, and I felt better for it.

Once Azaylia was properly awake and I started changing her nappy, I could see she wasn't feeling great today. She was niggling and looked quite aggravated, and she seemed to be in discomfort.

'Mummy will make you as comfy as she can,' I promised. 'Let's get you clean and dressed, shall we?'

The nurse checked her over and there was nothing in particular to worry about; she was just having an off day and we should carry on and make the best of it.

I'd bought lots of different Christmas outfits for Azaylia so we could take plenty of photographs and make as many memories as possible. Ashley and me were dressing up as Santa and Mrs Claus to make it lovely for Azaylia and we also had matching red and white pyjamas for all three of us. This was going to be a rare opportunity to have photos taken together. I'd planned to make the most of every second, but we'd have to see how Azaylia was feeling first.

I put her in a cosy vest with a white fairy outfit over the top and she seemed to brighten up a little.

'Do you want to open a present, Azaylia? Do you?'

I offered her a beautifully gift-wrapped parcel and got Ashley on FaceTime. He was desperate to see her little face and was grinning from ear to ear – 'How is she? What's she doing?'

'She's about to open a present,' I said.

We both watched as she tore at the wrapping paper, completely ignored the gorgeous teddy bear inside and proceeded to play with the crinkly paper, scrunching it up to see what sound it made.

'Isn't that typical?' I said. 'She's found joy in the simplest thing. We should have bought her a roll of wrapping paper instead!'

'Brilliant!' Ashley said. 'I love it! Daddy can't wait to see you, Azaylia!'

When Ashley arrived a few hours later, he was already in his Santa outfit. I nipped back to the hotel to have a shower and dress up as Mrs Claus and, when we were back in the room together, we sat down and had some food. One of our followers had sent chicken and chips and rice boxes to the hospital, and a cake and a big hamper had also been delivered for us.

'This feels naughty,' I giggled as I tucked in.

'What, being dressed as Santa and Mrs Claus?'

'No! Being in this room together. Eating food. It's so odd. I feel like we're going to get told off.'

Azaylia was napping in her cot, and when she woke up and needed a nappy change, Ashley and me both jumped up at the same time.

'So who's gonna do it?' he laughed. 'Fight ya for it!'

Throughout Azaylia's time in hospital, we'd both been acting as part-time single parents. We had just got on with it – we had no choice – and it was so strange to be together like this.

I was really enjoying myself. Ashley put Christmas music on, there was a happy vibe in the room and, best of all, Azaylia had perked up and seemed better than she did first thing.

We had a small blow-up bed in the room by now. I ordered it from Argos because Ashley and me both desperately needed a more comfortable place to sleep than the red chair and nobody seemed to object. Ashley's mum, Vicky, had made a trifle for us and I sat Azaylia on my lap on the bed on the floor and put the bowl in front of the three of us. Azaylia was suddenly much brighter now and she kept leaning forward and opening her mouth wide, trying to have a taste of the trifle. We let her have a tiny bit of the cream and she was going mad for it.

'Her head's gonna end up in that trifle in a minute!' we said. Me and Ashley were laughing our heads off and Azaylia was licking her lips and having an absolute ball – it was the best moment of Christmas Day by a mile.

The clock was ticking, but before it was time for me to leave, me and Ashley dressed in all our different outfits and had loads of pictures taken. It was fun. We danced and we sang together, and I felt like a proper mum, having done so much preparation behind the scenes, like all mums do.

'All I want for Christmas is you,' I started to sing to Azaylia, feeling every word. As I sang, Mariah Carey popped up on the TV, belting out her Christmas hit. The song had been following me around for weeks and it had started to feel like I was meant to hear it and it was 'our' song – mine and Azaylia's. The lyrics were so apt. If I could swap everything and anything I had for Azaylia's health and recovery, I would. She really was all I wanted, and I would give my own life so she could live hers, if that were possible.

Our two hours were up all too soon, but that was all we were allowed because of the Covid restrictions and we had to stick to the strict rule. I found it really, really hard when I had to say goodbye to Azaylia, although when I walked out of Ward 18 I didn't see the oxygen tanks and NG tubes, or the bald heads and sunken eyes that sometimes followed me down the corridor. All I saw were happy, smiling faces, bobbing heads covered with colourful paper hats and parents who seemed to have grown six inches, the weights on their shoulders cast aside, just for today. That helped lift my spirits a little, though I was still very upset to leave Azaylia on Christmas Day.

Ashley's mum Vicky, his sister Alissia, my brother Danny and Ashley's auntie Michelle had driven over to see me at the hotel so I wasn't on my own, but even so I felt incredibly sad.

'Next year it'll be different,' I told them. 'Next year we'll have a proper family Christmas.'

• • •

Before we were given the news that we had a bone marrow match for Azaylia, ITV came to interview us about our donor appeal, filming us on a bench outside the hospital on a bitterly cold day. I was terrified of rabbiting on and not getting my point across and I was also incredibly nervous because the report was going out nationally and I'd never done anything like it before.

I was wearing a beige coat and my hair was blowing all over the place. Ashley suddenly started sneezing, which meant we had to stop filming so he could blow his nose. *We must look such a mess*, I thought, *but so what?*

The important thing was that we got our story across. The appeal was still very much on and this was an amazing opportunity to get more potential donors signing up. It was, quite literally, a matter of life and death and this report could potentially benefit thousands of people as well as our daughter.

This is for you, champ! I said to myself as I stood in front of the camera and it really wasn't that difficult. Azaylia would have done a brilliant job if she could do it herself and I just had to be strong and brave like her.

The interview was due to go out just after Christmas and we were told we'd be the top item on the ITV Midlands news. On 27 December 2020 I switched on the TV on the wall in Azaylia's room and waited. And then I waited some more.

Prime Minister Boris Johnson had an announcement to make, about lockdown, and after that, there was an interview with Secretary of State for Health and Social Care Matt Hancock, followed by an item about the now former US president Donald

Trump, who'd signed a new Covid relief and government funding bill.

'Well, how come all those people get on the telly before you, Azaylia?' I said. 'That's not right, is it? I was joking, of course. We were still in a global pandemic and it was hardly surprising there was so much news. 'Oh, hold on, there you are!'

The reporter had used some of our own video footage and there was Ashley holding Azaylia up in the air in her room and me playing with her, alongside Simba and Nala on the bed. In one of the clips Azaylia was dressed in a Christmas sleepsuit with snowmen on the sleeves and she looked so pretty with a red head-band on her head. My heart overflowed with love for her.

In the weeks since our appeal launched, a total of more than 80,000 people had joined the registers to be potential donors. It was a phenomenal figure – 80,000! I felt so incredibly proud of Azaylia and all the donors. The reporter had asked us what message we wanted to give to people out there.

'Keep being incredible!' I said to Azaylia now, echoing the words I was speaking on TV.

I was so happy with how the report had gone. We'd succeeded in getting our message across, which meant so many more lives could be saved.

What a Christmas present that was.

CHAPTER THIRTEEN

'Let's go, champ! Come on, champ!'

Azaylia was finally starting the transplant process and I was allowed to sit with her for part of the treatment. Transfusing the donated blood into her body would only take about ten to fifteen minutes because of her size and the small amount of blood she was receiving. Ashley and me had agreed to share the time at her side, so everything was divided up 50:50, as always.

Azaylia had lost all her hair now and had no eyebrows or eyelashes, but she looked so serene and courageous as she lay in a hospital bed, her eyes wide open. She was even trying to smile. It blew my mind.

'Go on, Azaylia!' I said. 'You're doing so well! Look at you!'

This felt like the biggest day of our lives. We'd been wishing and hoping and praying for this moment for so long and it had been such a rocky road to get this far. Despite the fact we were told they'd found a potential donor for Azaylia back in December

2020, there were lots of tests to be done and so many things that could have gone wrong, right up until this moment.

When we went public with an update on Azaylia's transplant, we wanted to give positive news to our followers and to all the people who'd signed up to the donor registers. That meant waiting until the last minute when we knew for certain the transplant was going ahead. Now we'd finally put the news on social media and it was so uplifting: we had the green light and there was no going back.

The specialists could not have prepared us better for what to expect. We'd been warned that the room where the transfusion took place would smell of sweetcorn because of the preservative in the bone marrow and the smell would come out of Azaylia's skin afterwards too. Every detail had been passed on to us and I felt empowered by all the education and information I soaked up. I was so grateful, because knowledge helped me feel more in control of myself, and the situation.

I briefly filmed Azaylia having the transfusion, not just as a personal record of her journey, but also because I wanted to share it on Instagram. The support and love we got from our followers meant so much and this was a way of not just keeping them updated, but giving something back. If I'd been able to see a video like this when I found out Azaylia needed a transplant, it would have been a massive help. As it was, I'd gone through such a steep learning curve and now I had so much to share.

By now I had close to a million followers, and Ashley had over a million. *My videos could potentially help other people*, I thought, *so why not spend a few minutes of my day doing them?* If it helped one person, that would be amazing.

Blogging had become a welcome distraction for me too and it was also a kind of therapy. I didn't want to sit and dwell on what might go wrong during the transplant process and writing positive, motivational words always helped lift my spirits.

We'd moved Club 100 from Ward 18 to Ward 19. Azaylia was now having the life-saving treatment she needed, and therefore being on Ward 19 was a huge step forward. Ashley and me were sticking firmly to the optimistic script we'd been following for more than three months. We were on the next stage of her journey and we would continue to surround her with positivity and love and as much happy energy as we could muster. This transplant was going to save her life. That's what we told each other, and that's what I told any demons in my head who dared to approach me in the dark and tell me anything otherwise.

• • •

We'd been allowed to take Azaylia home for two short stays, once back in December and then for a whole week at New Year, both times when she was on a break from chemo and awaiting the next stage of her treatment. Carrying her out of the hospital and putting her in the car after so many months inside was very odd. I felt proud and excited and nervous and scared, all at the same time. She had been wrapped in a bubble for so long and it seemed so weird to be out in the real world with her, driving her along a motorway as if everything was perfectly normal.

As soon as we got through our front door I felt as if my emotions were strung out behind me, all the way from Birmingham to Nuneaton. I was excited about all the normal stuff we could do – even just giving Azaylia a bath in our own bathroom – and it was a huge relief to be surrounded by home comforts. I was looking forward to some privacy too, just being able to sit on the settee with Azaylia on my lap, Ashley by my side and no *beep-beep-beeping* or nurses running in. But there was an undercurrent of anxiety I couldn't ignore. The consultant was going to tell us when we needed to return for more treatment, so we were on borrowed time, waiting for a call. And of course, we had a huge responsibility on our hands, caring for Azaylia's daily needs all by ourselves.

Before we left hospital, I'd made lists of all the things the nurses were checking every day. I replicated it at home, covering the kitchen cupboards with Post-it notes so I knew exactly what I needed to do and when. We'd been taught how to give Azaylia her feed and medicines down her lines and use her milk machine, and the head nurse had to sign off our training before we were discharged. The medicine went into her NG tube via a syringe and you had to flush it down with some sterilised water afterwards before reconnecting the same tube to Azaylia's feed. We managed really well. Even so, it was stressful having no back-up or emergency buzzer, just in case something went wrong.

At night we instinctively took turns to sleep, neither of us daring to leave Azaylia unwatched. Sometimes, in the middle of the night, I would look at her sleeping and my mind would wander to places I didn't want it to go. Azaylia was such a sick little girl, what if she took a turn for the worse? What if we had to call an ambulance and it took too long to come? At moments like that, I felt desperate to get her back in hospital and to push on with her treatment without delay.

The family had been keeping an eye on our house and it looked exactly as it had when we left it months earlier. They'd filled the fridge and cleaned and tidied and made it very welcoming for us. I was so grateful to them, but however lovely it all was, there was a painful truth staring me in the face every day: this was not the kind of homecoming we wanted. *Nothing* was how we wanted it.

Azaylia's bedroom was as pristine as the day we left for Manchester. It wasn't meant to be like that. All of her new toys should be here, spilling out of her toy box. I opened her wardrobe and stole a look inside. The six- and twelve-month-plus clothes were still hanging up.

We'll be back by the time they fit you, Azaylia. Don't you worry, princess.

Our close family members came to the front window to say hello, bringing their kids and having little get-togethers. When my brother brought Noah, it was incredibly emotional: 'Look, Azaylia,' I said brightly. 'It's your cousin! You'll be able to play with him soon!'

Everyone had so much love and warmth and affection to give, even seeing them through glass filled me with so much joy. They clapped and danced and sang and Azaylia watched them all with a fantastic mixture of enthusiasm and curiosity written all over her face. Friends and family were pining to hold Azaylia again. Nobody had got to hold her since she was eight weeks old, but if this was all we could do for now, we'd make the most of it.

'I brought you this.'

It was Danny, holding up a chicken biryani his friend's mum had made and a cup of chai tea from Chai Wala, both my favourites. I felt so much love for him. He'd been an absolute rock and I wanted to cry when I watched him walk away, little Noah bouncing along beside him, full of life and innocence. My sister-in-law Michelle was there too. They should have been in our house. We should have been eating together and being one big, happy family, all enjoying life without fear and pain and this endless anxiety.

I was well aware that people all over the UK were only seeing their loved ones through windows or on FaceTime or Zoom. It was tough for everyone, but the lockdowns were expected to come to an end soon. As 2020 came to a close, most people were looking forward to life returning to normal, or something close to normal, before too long. But our family was facing so many extra layers of uncertainty. When would normality return for us? When would Azaylia be able to play with Noah and her new cousin Anaya? There was her two-year-old cousin Carmelo too, who is the son of Ashley's brother Ryan and my sister-in-law Nieki. We'd taken a photo of Vicky smiling proudly with her three little grandchildren before Azaylia became ill, which now felt like a lifetime ago.

I remembered the day Matty's girlfriend Amy and me changed the two girls on the bed together, giggling about how we were on nappy duty instead of partying like we used to. It had felt like our lives were on a parallel track, but look at us now, I thought. It was shocking to think how much had changed and how much we'd all been through since then.

. . .

At the very end of December, Azaylia had two procedures in preparation for her transplant. The first was bone marrow aspiration, which meant taking fluid and tissue from her spine to check there were no signs of cancer there. She was also given an additional central line, which was tunnelled under her skin just above her heart. That would be used to give chemotherapy and other medicines – the list would increase massively.

I always hated it when Azaylia was sedated. My heart ached when I saw the gas being wafted under her little nose. She looked so helpless and vulnerable, which wasn't the Azaylia I knew. When she went into theatre and I had to wait in a separate room I felt as if I'd lost a part of me. Azaylia *was* a part of me. That's one of the things you learn when you become a mother. The maternal bond is indescribably tight and you are forever bound to your baby, whatever the distance between you.

These were horrible, invasive procedures and now we would have to wait up to two weeks for the results of the bone marrow aspirate. Two weeks was a *very* long time to wait.

I barely slept a wink that night, even though both procedures went as smoothly as possible. I was worrying about whether Azaylia was in pain and if she would be suffering when she woke up. Thankfully, as usual, the morning light made everything seem a little bit better. Azaylia was comfortable and stable, and she had recovered well from the two surgeries, thank God.

It was New Year's Eve and we were given the green light to go home again, for a full week this time. Our little princess would get to see in the New Year at home with Mummy and Daddy, and that was an amazing gift.

'Thank you for being so brave and strong,' I told Azaylia, dressing her in a pink knitted two-piece outfit ready for the car journey.

I was incredibly grateful we were going home together, but as we turned into our road, I felt a weight swing around my heart. The time of year was haunting me, I realised. Images of other New Years flashed in front of me. Happy nights when we'd partied without a care in the world and been full of nothing but hope and expectation about the future. That's what New Year was about, or should be about.

We didn't celebrate in any of the normal ways. We just sat together at home, appreciating spending time with our daughter. Our lives would not start again – not properly – until Azaylia was through the transplant and in remission from her cancer.

Late into the evening Azaylia accidentally pulled her NG tube out and we had to dash up to University Hospitals Coventry and Warwickshire to have it put back in place. We finally returned to the car at 11.58pm. I waited for a couple of minutes before driving off, and as the clock struck midnight I held Azay-lia's hand and said a prayer to bring in the New Year. Ashley sat in the back seat with her as we headed home. At least we were all together, I thought.

On New Year's Day I had no space in my head to think about the kind of resolutions I normally made. I'd put on weight in hospital, but so what? I'd been comfort eating, but I gave no thought to my diet, or exercise. These days it was rare for me to do anything other than pile my hair on top of my head in a topknot. I was normally so invested in self-care. I know how important it is, but all of that could wait – it wasn't important to me right now.

Ashley had kept up his fitness and had been going to the gym when it was my turn in the hospital with Azaylia. Keeping fit was his therapy and he always felt better for it. He'd been turning away work for months and I wiped my client diary clean the day Azaylia was admitted to hospital. Our families had been fantastic in this regard, offering to help us out financially if we needed it. They insisted on paying some of our hotel bills and were constantly looking for other ways to help us out. Somehow they managed to have a fridge and microwave installed in our hotel room so we could store and cook the homemade food they deliv-ered, which was a massive help. Left to my own devices I'd have just carried on living off takeaway deliveries and snacks from the hospital shop and café.

The family came over and did window visits, like they did most days. They knew how fragile and scared we were feeling, but that didn't stop them shouting 'Happy New Year!', blowing kisses and being bright and bubbly. Matty and Amy brought Anaya, which was very moving. Anaya was thriving and glowing with health, and I was delighted to see her doing so well. But our two little princesses were meant to be growing up together, not seeing each other through a pane of glass, and all with Azaylia attached to tubes. I felt overwhelmed and I took a back seat while Ashley stood at the window with Azaylia. I had never, ever allowed pity into our lives and I never once asked 'why me?' or 'why us?' But just for a split second I could feel my pain rising. *Why couldn't our families be together in the way we imagined? How was this our fate?* I knew that if I gave those ideas any oxygen it would not help anyone, least of all Azaylia. I couldn't let any negative energy in and I had to step back and re-boot myself.

Ashley's mum brought pasta and chicken and salmon and salad and jacket potatoes. Everyone in the family was so support-ive, as were all our friends and neighbours. It was wonderful to be back in our own community, but even so, I didn't want to be in Nuneaton. I was counting down the days because, as soon as we got back to Birmingham, Azaylia's treatment would be moving forward and we'd be one step closer to coming home for good.

We'd been at home for a week when we finally got the call to return to the hospital. I was flooded with relief. 'Come on,' I said. 'This is it, Azaylia! Let's go!'

Club 100 had been disrupted during our time at home, but it was time to pump up the positivity as high as we could take it.

'Let's go, champ!' I whooped. 'It's time to go!'

● ● ●

'How are you doing, gorgeous girl?' I said. 'Look at you!'

Azaylia was gurgling away in her air-locked bedroom on Ward 19. She had moments when she looked so desperate to start talking and I couldn't wait for the day to come. She was doing amazingly well. Immediately after her transplant she'd had a long sleep and then watched her favourite cartoon show on my laptop, *CoComelon*. I dressed her in a vest that said 'I love my daddy' and she sat on my lap, chomping on a teething ring and playing with a big plastic yellow rattle. She seemed so happy and alert, and it didn't seem real that she'd had a life-saving transfusion that same day.

The doctors were pleased with her, though it wasn't lost on me that the simple fact Azaylia was still here was a measure of success. We could have lost her at any time during the transplant and here she was, glued to *CoComelon* and giving me smiles.

We still had a long road ahead. That was a phrase I'd got used to hearing in hospital. As we'd been told, Azaylia would need more chemotherapy as well as additional stem cell treatments and blood transfusions and, as we'd been warned at the start, the engraftment process could take several months or even a year. We might start to get an indication of how the engraftment was going in about two weeks, all being well, but we were probably looking at somewhere between four and nine months before we'd know exactly what percentage of engraftment she'd achieved.

Azaylia would have to stay in her sterile, air-locked room on Ward 19 throughout this time and we were warned to expect her condition to get worse before it got better. I couldn't really imagine it – she looked amazingly well – but that was Azaylia for you.

'She'll give you 100 per cent,' I told every single nurse who came to attend to her. They would look at me warily and warn me that we'd just have to wait and see. One member of the team said 90 per cent engraftment would be a good result and we could work with that. It didn't need to be 100, another said. It was rare to hit 100.

'No,' I said to every one of them. 'Trust me, she's gonna give us 100 per cent. Azaylia is so strong, her body's so receptive to treatment. I know she'll do it.'

In the days following the transplant, Azaylia experienced several side effects that we'd been told would come. She had mucositis, which made her mouth sore and inflamed, she had sickness and constipation and she suffered changes to her skin, which looked dry and sunburnt on her back, under her armpits and in all her little creases. I wanted to wave a magic wand and make it all go away. I couldn't, so I made myself as useful to her as possible, keeping her clean and fresh, trying to stimulate her mind and, most of all, making sure she knew she was loved and cared for, and that me and Daddy were rooting for her every step of the way.

I bathed Azaylia every morning while her room was cleaned down and it became my favourite part of the day. I put music on, danced and sang along and then held her close in a big fluffy blanket. It was such a simple pleasure, but our situation had changed my perspective on life. I appreciated every precious moment like that and I thanked God and the universe for letting me be a mummy and giving me the little miracle I held in my arms.

Azaylia had observations every four hours and the lists I'd created to keep track of all her stats and meds had now expanded hugely. She was on anti-sickness medication, anti-fungal and anti-rejection drugs as well as pain relief and medication for her liver. There was so much to learn and I made a board and drew charts so I could see for myself what her haemoglobin and platelet levels were, what meds she was having when, and all the other things the nurses were monitoring at regular intervals every day.

Once Azaylia engrafted, the aim would be to lower her medications to the point where she could have them orally, rather than through her central line. That would be taken away and then finally she could be discharged from hospital and return as an outpatient. That was the dream and that was the vision I kept at the forefront of my mind every minute of every day.

There was one very big, black cloud obscuring the view, one I'd shooed out of my head while Azaylia was having the transplant, along with the terrifying warnings we'd had about the complications she might suffer during the treatment, or the fact she could contract a fatal infection afterwards.

I knew I had to keep myself 100 per cent positive while she underwent the transplant, but I was catching my breath now and peering outside the protective bubble I'd wrapped myself in.

The reality was Azaylia's leukaemia was so aggressive that some cancerous cells had returned in the short window between her second round of chemo and starting the transplant process. We were told this in advance of the transplant and, when the words hit me, I felt physically winded. It took all of my strength to eventually be able to stand and walk out of the doctor's room.

Ashley and me had stared at each other in the corridor, neither of us speaking. It took me back to the moment we got the call to say Azaylia had to go to A&E immediately. Utter disbelief and shock pricked every pore and we could find no words to even begin to describe how we felt.

We had been praying for Azaylia to be clear of cancer when she went into her transplant. That had been the aim and that is what we believed would happen. Then, when she was engrafted, her new 'head gasket' would make nothing but healthy cells. She would finally be cured and we could all start living again. That was what was meant to happen, but it wasn't to be.

We'd put on a brave face going into the transplant; there was no point in doing anything else. Chemo had worked before and it would work again, that's what we had to believe. But now here we were again, asking for another miracle.

What if we can't get rid of the cancer? What then?

Thoughts like that prodded me when I was alone at night, but I always did my best to fight them off.

No, you can't think like that. Azaylia is strong. Azaylia will win! The chemo will wipe away all the cancer. She's a winner. It's all gonna work, every last bit of Azaylia's treatment. You'll see!

I wished I didn't have to spend every night alone. Sometimes, in the early hours when I couldn't sleep, I scrolled through Ashley's Instagram, knowing I would find comfort and inspiration.

'You are strong, you are mighty, you are courageous and God is with you!' he had posted, in response to the latest bad news. 'You got this Likkle Lion. We love you! LET'S GO CHAMP!'

I felt my heart lift. I could hear Ashley talking and I could see the fight in his eyes. His posts always motivated me to be more positive and to keep fighting. Like a beacon of hope, he never, ever stopped shining. When things got worse, he became stronger and shone brighter than before, just like Azaylia.

I said my prayers, like I always did, and I begged with all my heart and soul for Ashley to be right. Azaylia had this, of course Azaylia had this.

CHAPTER
FOURTEEN

There was a big silver bell on the wall of the long corridor leading away from the children's cancer ward. It was attached to a blue cloud-shaped sign emblazoned with a bright rainbow and underneath it read, 'Ring this bell three times well, its toll to clearly say, my treatment's done, this course is run and I am on my way'. Underneath was the inscription 'Irve Le Moyne'.

I'd looked at that bell so many times over the past four months and I'd heard other children ringing it to celebrate reaching the end of their treatment – *One day it'll be you, Azaylia*, I always thought.

Irve Le Moyne was a US Navy SEAL and he started the tradition in 1996, installing a bell at the American centre where he himself had been treated for cancer. There were now thousands of bells like this all over the world, waiting for children like Azaylia to ring them as they went on their way, back to normality and the life they should be living.

It was such a good idea and I loved hearing the bell ring out. It was a reminder there was always light at the end of the tunnel. Azaylia would get her turn, that's what I always believed, all the way along. One day, we'd be walking out of the hospital and putting all of this trauma and heartache behind us. Azaylia's leukaemia would be cured and we would finally be able to get on with the rest of our lives, just as we were always meant to.

We were in the engraftment stage now, and some mornings Azaylia looked so tired and ill. Her skin was very pale and she had red blotches around where her eyebrows should be, but she wasn't nearly as poorly as we'd been warned she might be. It was too early to know, but I was convincing myself she was engrafting well and was only sick because of the chemo she was having – it was doing its job, and that's all that was making her ill.

Ten days post-transplant, the doctors told us they were putting Azaylia on a TPN feed, because she wasn't tolerating being fed through her NG tube as usual. This meant having a bag of nutrients dripped directly into her veins through her central line, to make sure she was getting exactly what she needed.

'Right,' I said. 'You know what we're gonna do today, Azaylia?'

She was bright-eyed and had slept well. I sat her in her pink Bumbo seat, put a bib on her and encouraged her to eat a spoonful of baby rice. She spent more time chewing her green plastic weaning spoon than eating the food, but even if she ate just one teaspoon of rice it would be a step in the right direction. And guess what? She did it! One day she'd be eating all by herself. There would be no TPN and no NG tube, and the more she did for herself now, the easier it would be for her when she got to go home for good.

I had the same attitude when it came to helping Azaylia sit up unaided. She was dribbling a lot because she was still suffering with mucositis, but she had a determined glint in her eye as I encouraged her.

'Come on, you can do it,' I said. 'You can do anything you put your mind to, Azaylia. I know you can.'

I placed her toy piano in front of her. 'Look, baby! If you sit up, you can play it with your hands instead of your feet.'

Bless her, after several attempts, when she wobbled back into her pillows, she finally sat up all by herself for the very first time.

'What a clever girl!' I said, my heart exploding with pride and hope. 'What a milestone you've hit today!'

. . .

The nurses were teaching us all about Azaylia's new routines and medicines so we'd be fully prepared to take over when she was eventually discharged. It was a good sign, but we knew we couldn't read too much into this. Azaylia was still engrafting and we didn't yet have the results of her latest round of chemo. She was being tested all the time for one thing or another – her heart, her liver, everything. The care she was receiving was second to none, but there were no guarantees and the fact was she could still be in hospital for months on end.

After just a few weeks Azaylia looked as bright as a button nearly every day, which was such a boost. Sensing a shift in her, I felt very optimistic. It was February now and a month had gone by since her transplant.

'She's looking so strong and so good,' I said to Ashley outside the hospital one day. 'She'll be ringing that bell before we know it. She's turned a corner, I'm sure of it.'

'Yeah, we'll be home soon,' he replied casually, suddenly giving me a cheeky look. 'So who's gonna have the ensuite bathroom?'

It was such an unexpected comment. 'What? What are you talking about?'

'Me!' he replied. 'I'm having it!'

'What?'

'I'm serious,' he teased. 'I've decided that's gonna be my sanctuary. I've got used to having my own space, I need a sanctuary.'

'No way! I want that bathroom, you're not having it all to yourself!'

'I'll race you for it!' he challenged.

'OK!' I started running down the road as fast as my legs would take me. 'I win!' I laughed. 'I win!'

We hadn't messed about like that for so long. It was two minutes out of our day, but it lifted me for hours and hours. There was so much hope in the air, I could sense it.

Ashley decided to shave his head one day. 'Look, we're twins now!' he said as he walked into Azaylia's room. 'Do you like it?'

She properly giggled, giving a grin that was even cheekier than her daddy's. This was the Azaylia we knew so well, playing and smiling and shining her light around the room. He showed me the video of it afterwards and it was another moment that raised my spirits and gave me a glow inside. We had this. Our daughter was on the up and there was no way she was going back down.

On Valentine's Day I dressed Azaylia in a pretty white and red vest that said 'Azaylia Loves Daddy'. She looked absolutely adorable, posing happily for a picture. This was the type of thing I'd dreamed of doing when I was expecting Azaylia and felt so proud to be her mummy. I hadn't let any special dates pass by unnoticed. We had to keep hoping and praying and creating the happiest energy we could, and it seemed to be working wonders.

•   •   •

Within five weeks of Azaylia's transplant we were called to a meeting with some of the doctors. I could tell by the vibes in the room that this was going to bring positive news and I was right. I was gripping the chair and staring at the specialist intently as he told us she had engrafted.

I held my breath. 'Has she given us 100 per cent?'

The doctor smiled. 'Yes, she has.'

I cheered like a football fan watching their team score the winner and Ashley was punching the air and jumping up and down. 'We told you! That's our girl! She's a champ! We knew she'd do it! And in five weeks! *Five weeks*!'

I'd learned enough by now to know that you're strapped into a rollercoaster in hospital and that, even when you are given great news like this, you can never be sure where the next bend will take you. Azaylia had had another bone marrow aspiration and we were still waiting for the results of that to see if it came back cancer-free. We expected it would, given how well she'd responded to chemo in the past, but it was way too early for celebrations.

Still, this was incredible news. We'd been preparing to stay on Ward 19 for up to a year and it was only February. What an absolute legend Azaylia was! I could hardly let myself take it all in. We were one step closer to being able to take her home, at long last. She was six months old and she'd climbed mountain after mountain after mountain. Her little body had been through more than seemed humanly possible, but she'd soldiered on and she was winning, just like we always said she would.

I cried with happiness when I relayed the good news to the family. 'This journey is very nearly done,' I said to my brother. 'This is it now, this is the final stage.'

Once we got the results of the bone marrow aspiration, there would be nothing left in front of us, nothing more we had to face. I could feel Danny's relief pouring down the phone and everyone who heard the news shed a tear.

A few days later, when some of the medical team did their daily visits, I was told Azaylia could potentially be discharged in just a couple of days and that I should prepare the house for her return. After all we'd been through, it was a surprisingly casual, low-key conversation. This was a moment that called for a fanfare and balloons and music and dancing, I thought, my mind already racing forward in time to the celebrations we'd have once Azaylia was home.

'Does she get to ring the bell?' I asked.

'Of course,' a nurse said.

'Did you hear that, Azaylia? Are you gonna ring that bell? What a clever girl you are!'

Azaylia looked absolutely beautiful and strong too. She was gripping one of her rattles with all her might as she waved it above her head. Ashley always said she had strong hands – 'Tennis players' hands,' he said, again and again. He wanted to take her training, just like his grandfather took him to football training when he was a kid. She'd be an amazing tennis player one day. I'd heard it so many times, he never changed his tune about that.

Ashley always dreamed big and I loved him for it. I tried to match his passion and optimism every day, but when Azaylia was very poorly there were times when I found it incredibly painful to even think about the future. It was terrifying to think about what it might hold and on days like that I took all my hopes and dreams and bound them tightly to my heart. I wanted to guard them there and keep them very close, because then they couldn't make me sad or frightened or catch me unawares.

When I was pregnant, we imagined what it would be like going to Azaylia's parents' evenings in the future. I'd confessed to Ashley that I used to only behave in school in the week leading up to parents' evening, in the hope that the teachers would forget all about the fact I giggled and talked and messed about in class the rest of the time.

'I wonder if she'll be like me?' I laughed. 'Can you imagine you and me sitting there together, in front of her teachers. What if she's naughty? What would we say?'

Ashley was laughing his head off. I still felt like we were a couple of kids and so the idea of doing something as grown-up as going to a parents' evening seemed so alien and funny.

Later on in my pregnancy, we talked about how we both wanted to support and direct Azaylia in her life. Neither of us had a nine-to-five job and we both felt very strongly that we wanted to pass on our attitude to work. If you're ready to go to work, go to work, we would say. If you're not academic, don't worry about it. If you don't want to be a tennis player, don't be one. We both agreed we would tell our daughter the world was her oyster and she didn't have to tick boxes or conform to any societal pressures; she could carve out whatever life she wanted for herself. I hadn't revisited these conversations in such a long time, but suddenly the dreams of the future were unwrapping themselves from my heart and fizzing in my brain. The world *was* Azaylia's oyster and there was an incredible future waiting for her and for all of us.

· · ·

Preparing for Azaylia's return home was a big job. Thanks to the nurses we knew exactly what we had to do to take care of her medical needs at home, but there was still a lot to do. Azaylia's immune system was weak and she would be very susceptible to infection, which meant the house had to be as clean and sterile as possible and free from all dust.

That afternoon, as soon as Ashley arrived, instead of getting a rest at the hotel like I normally did, I drove straight home and started cleaning the house from top to bottom. I was literally on my hands and knees, wiping down the skirting boards and every other surface with Clinell wipes. I didn't stop for hours on end and by the time I went back to swap with Ashley the next day, I'd done twelve hours of cleaning and the house was shining like a new pin.

Azaylia had been back home for a week when the day we'd been waiting for – 23 February 2021 – finally arrived. Over the past seven days we'd been taking her back and forth for her appointments and now, after more than five months in hospital, she was being officially discharged and would become an outpatient. We needed to take her in for some blood tests that morning, and then we would carry her down the corridor between Wards 18 and 19 and help her ring the bell. It was the big moment she'd fought so hard for, and we were so excited and thankful on her behalf. As we got ourselves ready, me and Ashley were full of hope and anticipation.

'Can you believe it?' I said to Ashley. 'She's just gonna be an outpatient now. Is it really happening?'

'Yes!' he said. 'It really is. And this is all down to YOU, Azaylia.'

I dressed her in a comfy animal print babygro with a matching headband. We had everything planned. Ashley would carry her in his arms as we walked down the corridor and we'd both help Azaylia ring the silver bell.

After we arrived at the hospital we asked a member of staff to film the whole event for us, so we could share the happiness with our family and friends and, most of all, so we'd have a keepsake of the big day, to show Azaylia in the future.

She had her blood tests as planned, and then me and Ashley had a selfie taken with her, to mark the moment. Shortly afterwards, a member of Azaylia's medical team appeared.

'Can I have a word?'

It was just ten minutes before we were due to leave and dozens of nurses and other members of staff were already lining the corridor between Wards 18 and 19, waiting to clap and cheer as Azaylia rang the bell.

'Yes, of course.'

There was a note of urgency in the doctor's voice and she wasn't smiling, which immediately frightened me. Ashley was beside me and we both waited with bated breath for what the doctor was about to tell us.

'What is it?'

There was no easy way to say this, the doctor said, but the results of Azaylia's latest bone marrow aspiration had just come back, unexpectedly early, and it was not the good news we were expecting. My heart was thumping in my chest. I looked at Ashley, and he looked like he'd turned to stone. All the signs had been that Azaylia was cancer-free. Of course that was the case, you only got to ring the bell when your cancer was in remission. All her blood results, every other test. All of it had been clear. This test had been an additional one, I thought. They did another bone marrow aspiration just to double-check that everything really was as it should be. It was ticking the final box, wasn't it?

'What do you mean? What is it?'

Time was standing still. The bone marrow aspiration showed that Azaylia's body was still producing cancerous cells. In other words, her leukaemia had returned, despite the fact that her body had accepted the transplant so well.

My throat turned into a lump of rock and my stomach dropped like a broken elevator. How could this have happened? How had this moment been turned completely upside down, plunging us all into another nightmare? This was meant to be the start of the rest of our lives and now what?

I looked at Azaylia and my heart went out to her. She didn't deserve a setback like this, she deserved to ring the bell and leave this hospital cancer-free.

The doctor left us alone to decide what to do.

'Shall we go and tell everyone she's not ringing the bell?' I said.

Ashley didn't know what to say. 'I don't know, I just don't know. Everyone is waiting in the corridor. This is too much. All the family is waiting to celebrate ...'

He looked completely broken and neither of us could think straight. Two nurses came in. We could still take Azaylia home today and, if she still wanted to ring the bell on the way out, of course she could, after all she'd been through. They left us to think about it.

'What do you want to do, Safiyya?'

'We can't do it,' I said. 'We can't, can we?'

Ashley told the family what had happened and we started to gather ourselves together. We were on the verge of telling everyone to leave the corridor and just let us go home without any fuss, but at the very last moment, something stopped me. I wondered what Azaylia was thinking, and what she would do. When I turned to look at her, she gave me the most beautiful, angelic smile. It changed my mind completely.

'Look at that beautiful face,' I said. 'It's telling us the show must go on.'

Ashley nodded and said he agreed with me. After all, Azaylia had completed round after round of chemo and she'd engrafted 100 per cent. Of course she deserved to ring the bell. Our decision was made.

'Let's go, champ!' Ashley said. 'You gonna come and ring that bell with Mummy and Daddy?'

Walking down that corridor was incredibly hard. There hadn't been time for all the staff to be told the latest update and dozens of doctors and nurses and support staff were lined up, happy smiles on their faces. Their applause got louder and louder as we turned the corner and stood in front of the bell.

We both did our best to smile too. Ashley bent down to hold Azaylia in front of the bell – it was the height of a child on the wall – and I took hold of her little hand and helped her ring it.

Loud cheers went up, and Ashley and me were both fighting back tears despite the fact we were still trying to keep smiling. We were both wearing masks, which was a blessing. Nobody could see that I was biting my lips, though Ashley's eyes said it all. He was being as courageous and strong as ever, but he'd been blindsided in the worst possible way and he looked confused and absolutely devastated.

Azaylia started crying at the sound of the bell and Ashley bounced her in his arms and held her aloft. 'Come on, champ,' he said. 'Listen, it's onto the next part of your journey now, baby.'

A nurse appeared and presented Azaylia with a certificate, 'for being with us, and completing your journey'. I had hold of Azaylia now and I cuddled her close. She'd completed her transplant journey and she deserved this moment, I thought to myself, smiling at the nurse and thanking all the staff.

I wanted to leave as quickly as possible, but Ashley did the right thing and stopped to say a few words. 'Thank you for all the care you've given us,' he said. 'For looking after Azaylia, and the care for us, as parents. It's been amazing.' His words were sticking in his throat and I felt so proud of him for taking the time to do this. Neither of us wanted to stay a minute longer. We wanted to get Azaylia home, process what had just happened and find out what the next stage of Azaylia's treatment would be.

Ashley bravely carried on. 'We got some news today,' he told everyone. 'That Azaylia's leukaemia has come back, but that just means we stay positive, like we've been all the way through.' He said he hoped she'd get to ring the bell again soon, so we could finally get out of the hospital once and for all.

'Let's go, champ!' I said, raising Azaylia's right arm in the air to signal the end of the show.

Ashley had been incredibly strong and dignified, but it was time to go now.

CHAPTER
FIFTEEN

'This is by far the saddest and most heartbroken I have ever been.'

We were back home, sitting on the settee with Azaylia asleep in her car seat by the front door. I turned to look at Ashley. It wasn't like him to speak this way, but before I could reply, he added: 'And it's also the happiest and most complete I've ever been.'

He'd taken Azaylia for a stroll with his brother Matty and his best mate Anthony and their two little girls, Anaya and Willow. He'd come back looking positive, despite the sadness in his heart. I totally understood his mixed feelings.

We'd both changed so much since becoming parents and Azaylia's illness had given us a totally new perspective on the world. Spending time together was the most precious thing we could possibly have and, even in these circumstances, we cherished moments like this. We had so much to be thankful for and, however much heartache we were going through, every day with Azaylia was a blessing.

It was *wonderful* to be back home, doing normal things outside of a clinical environment. Our days were busy, attending to Azaylia's every need, giving her all her various medicines and keeping the house spotlessly clean. Azaylia was still susceptible to infection and even Ashley was running around dusting and cleaning. 'Miracles do happen!' I teased. The paint was wearing thin on the woodwork because we cleaned it so much, the leather on the back of the sofa cracking and peeling because it was wiped down and sterilised that many times.

Azaylia loved being in her Minnie Mouse bouncer and she was unbelievably happy and smiley every day. When she went out in her pram we had to make sure she was completely sealed inside, so no dust or pollution could get in, because there was building work going on at a house over the road. Still, Azaylia was gurgling away contentedly in her little bubble, bashing her rattles and making as much noise as she could.

I dealt with any negativity that crept up in the same way I dealt with dust. I was sweeping it away, not one speck of it was getting in. That's what Azaylia was doing. She was fighting and smiling, and I followed her lead, despite the next set of obstacles we had to face.

Azaylia would return to hospital as an outpatient now. The first step was to reduce the cyclosporine medication she was on, which was helping to regulate her new stem cells. The doctors were hoping that the stem cells would then get a boost and start to fight off her leukaemia cells themselves, at full force. After that she'd have another bone marrow test, which meant going into theatre again for another spine aspiration, and then we'd face another wait of up to two weeks for the results to see if she was finally cancer-free. The consultants told us that, if she still had leukaemia after that, there were few options left and chemo wouldn't help this time. This was a footnote, but we didn't dwell on it: she was going to get the all-clear this time, we were convinced of it.

· · ·

After a couple of weeks at home it was Mother's Day. Ashley took a lovely photo of me kissing Azaylia's hand while she sat in her pink and white high chair. It's a picture I cherish – we were looking at each other with so much love in our eyes.

'Being at home and enjoying this special day with you is the best gift I could get,' I posed on Instagram, sharing the picture. 'The simple moments like breakfast time with u fill my heart with warmth. Azaylia u have taught me so much over these past months, a few being strength, courage & belief. I pray and thank god every day for making me a mommy.'

Afterwards, she lay on her beanbag and Ashley tickled her feet. 'Pooh! Stinky feet!' he said as she kicked her feet under his nose. He blew a raspberry on her belly and she gave her beautiful little giggle. As I drank in every moment, I could almost feel myself drawing strength from Azaylia – she was radiating positive energy and it was keeping us all alive.

We went back to hospital twice a week to have Azaylia's bloods taken and all her observations done, as well as seeing the dietician and letting the consultant check her over. Life felt more normal than it had in months and months, although we were still waiting for the Azaylia's bone marrow results to come back, so we were holding our breath every single day.

It'll be fine, I told myself. *Look at her! She's thriving.*

Even so, every night I said my prayers, and every night I asked for the results to bring us good news, at last.

We were called to a meeting with one of the consultants and I felt myself being buckled into that rollercoaster once again, not knowing which way this was going to go.

It'll be fine, I repeated to myself. *There can be no more shocks. Please, let there be no more shocks.*

The spine aspiration results were back, we were told.

'Please, take a seat.'

Once again, the body language and the energy in the room broke the news to us before the doctor did. And once again, there was no easy way to say this, and no way of dressing it up.

The news was devastating: Azaylia still had leukaemia, despite the success of her transplant.

'What?'

The words were sliding down my brain, sticking like tar and making my whole mind turn black. I felt my heart rate spike and, all over my body, my skin felt like it had had been turned inside out, exposing every nerve ending to the elements. Visibly distraught, Ashley dropped his head into his hands and cried.

'How can she still have cancer after everything she has been through? How?'

His words hung in the air.

• • •

We'd been told there would be very few options left if we found ourselves in this position, but that meant there was still hope, didn't it? Only *no* options meant no hope.

We came out fighting. What exactly were the options? What could we do now to save our little girl?

The doctors told us there was nothing more that could be done in Birmingham, or anywhere in the UK, but we didn't give up hope. Another mother had reached out to me on social media, telling me that her son had benefited from treatment in Singapore that was not available in the UK. She had been told there was no hope at all for her child, but he was still alive today.

Despite the fact I'd been telling myself Azaylia's latest results would surely be clear, I knew there was a risk it might go the other way and we'd been quietly looking into Singapore, just in case. The treatment was called CAR-T therapy and in very simple terms, it targets specific markers that come back after a bone marrow test.

It was time to discuss it with Azaylia's medical team. Azaylia's markers were CD33 and CD34, and we quickly established that Singapore could potentially offer her the targeted treatment she needed. It was our very last hope. We trusted and respected her medical team completely, and we asked the doctors' opinion.

Was Azaylia well enough to travel to Singapore and would they support us in taking her there?

The answer was yes to both questions. Ashley and me had another one of those moments where the look in each other's eyes spoke without saying a word: *We've got this! We'll do whatever it takes. We'll fight to the ends of the earth for Azaylia.*

From that point on, our feet didn't touch the floor. Over the next few days we had long discussions with our consultants in the UK, as well as Zoom meetings with a professor in Singapore. In addition to the CAR-T therapy, Azaylia would need a haplo transplant, which is a bone marrow transplant using blood and stem cells donated from a close biological relative, typically a parent or sibling. We learned that the reason for this was that in Singapore they simply don't keep blood and stem cell banks the way we do in the UK. Fathers are the preferred parent, we were told, as the chances of the transplant being a success are higher when the donor is male.

We also discovered that, because of Covid, only one parent was allowed to travel to Singapore with Azaylia. My heart sank when I heard that. It felt like a kick in the teeth. We'd been together the whole time and now I could potentially be in Singapore for up to a year with Azaylia. If that's what we had to do, that's what we had to do. We had no choice. I would fly out to Singapore with Azaylia and Ashley would be the haplo donor, which at least meant he would be able to join us later.

We understood that we could lose our daughter at any time during the process. That was made very clear to us, right from the start. We'd been down this road before with her first transplant and it didn't come as a shock, but it was terrifying nonetheless. I could be alone with Azaylia if the worst happened and Ashley could be on the other side of the world; it didn't bear thinking about.

'We'll do it,' we said at every turn. 'We'll do whatever it takes.'

There was one very large fly in the ointment: the cost of the treatment started at £500,000 and we'd have to pay upfront just to be accepted onto the programme. Needless to say, we didn't have anything like that amount of money sitting around in the bank. Our families were incredible, immediately offering to re-mortgage their homes on top of giving us whatever savings they had, but there was no time for that – we needed the money right now.

There was only one way we could hope to raise the cash as quickly as we needed it and that was by launching an urgent appeal online and praying our followers and supporters came up trumps again. The bone marrow donor appeal had massively exceeded our expectations, what did we have to lose? We agreed that we would ask for donations to a GoFundMe in Azaylia's name, and see what the universe gave us. I was incredibly anxious and all sorts of doubts filled my head. Asking people we'd never even met to give money was a huge step. The country was in dire straits with Covid and families were queuing at food banks. Our followers had been absolutely fantastic and now they were like a giant family all around us, but even so, could we really expect them to put their hands in their pockets at a time like this?

Once again, it was looking at Azaylia's little face that gave us the strength and courage to move forward. Of course we would do this, we would do absolutely anything for Azaylia.

Writing the post was emotionally challenging for Ashley, but he did it absolutely beautifully: 'Azaylia has changed our lives, she has made our lives and she deserves the chance to live her own life,' he wrote. 'She is beautiful, she is strong, she is courageous and she glows with hope and happiness. Our hearts are intertwined and with one beat of her heart, our hearts beat along together. Please help our hearts continue to beat as one!'

I was so proud of Ashley. Azaylia had opened up a part of his heart I didn't know was there. 'We are on our knees asking for help to get us to Singapore,' he went on. 'Even the smallest of donations can help us reach our goal! Please help us to save our beautiful daughter Azaylia, she has inspired not only us as her parents but so many other people around the world. If you have been following our journey you can see that she shows us all every day how much she loves life and wants to be here! Please save. Please share. And please help us save our little girl.'

We'd worked flat out to get to this point and it was a big moment when we pressed the button and the appeal went live. It was only a matter of days since we'd been given the bad news, but time was not on our side and the clock was ticking, fast. We had a couple of weeks, maximum, to get Azaylia to Singapore. Her cancer had proven itself to be incredibly aggressive and, if we waited any longer, it would be too late.

I wanted to sit on my phone and never take my eyes off the GoFundMe page, but I was also nervous of what I'd see. I was sure we'd get plenty of positive messages about it on social media because our followers had been a phenomenal support through-out, but would anyone actually donate? It was a complete shot in the dark and what if it simply didn't work?

Ashley phoned me and he was buzzing. 'People are incredible,' he was saying. 'All of these people are supporting us. All of our followers. The public, the community, this is breathtaking!'

Money had started pouring in, he told me. A *lot* of money.

'Do you think we're gonna make it?' I said. My phone signal was weak inside the hospital and when I was with Azaylia I didn't really have time to keep checking on the website. 'What's going on?'

'Safiyya, you need to take a look. *She* has done this. Our baby has done this!'

Unbelievably, within three hours of the post going live we hadn't just got the £500,000 we needed, Azaylia had raised a million pounds.

'A million?' I said, completely gobsmacked. 'Is it really a million?' I could hardly believe it, but I was looking at my phone now and there it was, staring me in the face. The GoFundMe had rocketed above and beyond the target we set and the dona-tions were still coming in thick and fast, but there was no time to process the enormity of what had taken place, or to thank every single donor personally, which is what I wanted to do.

From that moment on, it was a race against the clock to get to Singapore. The nurses at Birmingham took Azaylia's bloods and sent them to a lab where samples were taken, put in compression tubes and couriered immediately to Singapore. As soon as they arrived, they would be tested to see if Azaylia's blood responded to the treatment in the way it needed to. Meanwhile, we were working round the clock, organising all the passports and paper-work as well as lining up flights and accommodation. And all the while, money kept flooding into the GoFundMe account. After twenty-four hours the total donated had reached an astonishing £1.4 million – it took our breath away.

'£1.4 million pounds, baby!' we said to Azaylia. 'Look what you've done! Look how much everyone loves you, baby!'

Azaylia was pale again, and niggly, but she still did her best to give us a little smile. That was her secret weapon, I thought. That's how my baby made all this magic happen, wasn't it?

So many donors had posted messages on the GoFundMe page and my heart melted when I started to look through them. There were thousands and thousands of messages, from all over the world. People were telling us Azaylia had changed the way they looked at life. They were parents and grandparents, sisters and brothers, cousins and aunties and uncles. Some gave their names and some stayed anonymous, but everyone was saying similar things. They praised Azaylia for smiling through every day with such courage and grace. She was an inspiration, they said, pledging whatever they could afford, even if it was just a couple of pounds.

Some of the very first donors were people Ashley or me knew or had worked with. The co-founder of PrettyLittleThing, Umar

Kamani, donated £20,000, which was absolutely amazing. In The Style's Adam Frisby gave an incredibly generous donation too, as did Mrs Hinch, aka Sophie Hinchliffe, and Molly-Mae Hague and Maura Higgins from *Love Island*.

'This is unreal!' Ashley was saying, scrolling through his phone. 'How are we ever gonna thank everyone?' Kate and Rio Ferdinand had also made very kind donations. We were totally blown away and for once it was not an understatement to say this meant the world to us, because Azaylia *was* our world.

The universe had not just responded to our plea, it had delivered more than we dared to dream of. So much goodness and positivity was pouring our way. It was just reward for all the sunshine and inspiration Azaylia had given to the world. Our daughter was going to go to Singapore and she was going to live.

• • •

A long time before the GoFundMe appeal had even been thought of, Ashley and me had talked about creating a charity in Azaylia's name. We'd learned so much on our journey and we wanted to give something back, helping other children with cancer and their families. The conversation had first started when we discussed how we wanted to keep raising awareness about blood and bone marrow donations, following the success of Azaylia's donor appeal.

'Imagine if we had a foundation,' we both thought, 'and when Azaylia is older, how amazing would it be if she could be an ambassador and help other children?'

It was a dream that had been floating around ever since and seeing the GoFundMe total rising so fast inevitably made us think about it again. We were in no position to give it the thought and attention it needed but, if we could raise so much money in such a short space of time, launching a charity surely had to be a goal we could achieve, when the time was right.

* * *

Azaylia was asleep in hospital when our oncologist came in with tears in her eyes. This particular doctor had been a powerhouse throughout our journey, offering endless support and encouragement. I'd never seen her like this before; she looked absolutely gutted. Every muscle in my body tightened and my breath was suspended in my lungs as I braced myself for what she had to say.

It was the worst possible news: Azaylia's blood had rejected the treatment in Singapore. Her leukaemia was spiking out of control and there was nothing else that could be done for her, anywhere.

I felt like everything was happening in slow motion.

We'd been defeated.

Our dreams were shattered.

There was nothing in the world we could do to save our little girl.

I sank to the floor. There had been many times when I felt I would fall to the ground but I never had, not until now. I couldn't stop it happening and I crouched in a ball and sobbed. I could hear Ashley crying up above me. Azaylia was just feet away, asleep in a cot. We had always vowed to be happy around her, but this time we simply couldn't stop our tears falling. I have no idea how long we stayed like that and the only thought that got me to my feet was that I wanted to see Azaylia's face, because I had to make the most of every second I had left with her.

A CT and ultrasound scan had shown that Azaylia had tumours in her brain, her kidneys, her liver and her spleen. There was no way of tackling the tumours on her brain because of the high pressure in her head and no amount of chemotherapy would cure her now – her leukaemia was far too widespread and aggressive.

'How long do we have?' Ashley croaked.

It was so painful to hear him speak those words. Nobody should have to ask a question like that.

There was a momentary pause. We could lose Azaylia at any time, we were told. She probably had just days to live. I looked at Ashley and he stared back, unblinking. How had so much hope been lost in such a frighteningly short space of time? It was such a shocking turnaround and, instead of going full steam ahead and dashing to the airport, we had to prepare ourselves straight away for the journey we never, ever wanted to take.

We didn't fall into each other's arms but our hearts connected. Only Ashley and me truly understood each other's pain. Nobody else loved Azaylia the way we did. We'd been bound so tightly together on this journey and we'd carry on as one, supporting each other all the way.

• • •

I wanted to take Azaylia home immediately. She'd spent enough of her life in hospital and I just wanted to wrap her in love and warmth in the privacy of our own home. If I could have picked her up and walked straight out of the hospital right that very minute I would have, but there were so many things to organise first.

Azaylia would be going home in an ambulance the next day. We'd have to put oxygen cylinders all around our home and, at our request, we'd be taking a stats machine to monitor her heart rate. We would do that at least every four hours, along with taking temperature checks, administering a long list of medications and giving Azaylia regular feeds through her NG tube.

'The palliative care team will come and see you once you are settled at home, and they will help you with end-of-life care.'

End-of-life care. The words were so hideous, I couldn't believe I was hearing them.

'OK,' I said, though I wanted to shout that this had nothing to do with us and they must have made some terrible mistake.

Azaylia was being checked over by a doctor in preparation for leaving hospital. She was lethargic and pale-skinned and she seemed to be uncomfortable, which was very difficult to see.

'Not long now, princess,' I was whispering. 'We'll be going home tomorrow.'

Despite her discomfort, Azaylia wasn't crying and she was looking at me and listening attentively. I told her she was going to get lots of cuddles from all the family when we got back. The

Covid rules would finally allow it and we no longer had to keep Azaylia in a sterile bubble.

'Everyone's going to come and see you,' I told her. 'Won't that be amazing?'

When the doctor came to talk to us we were expecting to be given the final instructions for her ongoing care and to be told what time Azaylia was being discharged but that wasn't what she had to say at all.

'I'm afraid it's possible Azaylia could pass tonight,' she said. 'If the family wants to say goodbye, you might want to let them know.'

So many blows had rained down on us and I think I must have switched back into the autopilot survival mode I was in when Azaylia was first admitted. My mind and body couldn't cope with the full reality of what was happening and parts of me shut down. They must have done, because despite the tears dripping down my cheeks, I dutifully did what the doctor suggested and got on my phone, letting the family know the situation and inviting them to come and say goodbye, just in case Azaylia didn't make it through the night.

It was no longer a question of which direction we'd be flung in next on this horrendous rollercoaster, but when the next stick of dynamite was being detonated on the track.

Ashley was numb with shock; we all were, but I didn't believe it was Azaylia's last night, I really didn't. Perhaps that's how I managed to phone the family and stay upright. Azaylia was not leaving tonight, I could feel it.

Our close family members started heading to the hospital, but I remained convinced that it was not Azaylia's time and, thank God, my instincts were proved to be right.

My little girl held on.

CHAPTER
SIXTEEN

We should have been ringing the bell again when we left the hospital. I'd never stopped believing that we would and the words on the plaque had stuck to my head like glue: 'Ring this bell three times well, its toll to clearly say, my treatment's done, this course is run and I am on my way.' I recited them in my head every time I walked down the corridor outside Ward 18, or heard another child ringing the bell in the distance. If I kept tight hold of the words, they were more likely to come true – that's what I hoped. But now we were carrying Azaylia to the ambulance, not giving that bell a second glance. It was 9 April 2021 and the worst thing in the world was coming to pass. We were taking Azaylia home, to make the most of the time we had left.

The following day Ashley was holding a sleepy Azaylia in his arms. His eyes were closed and he was kissing her on the forehead while I gently guided her foot into the pot of liquid plaster.

We'd decided to have bronze castings made of Azaylia's hands and feet, and a lady had come to the house to make the mouldings. Despite what had happened on her last night at hospital, and the fact we were busily making keepsakes, I still wasn't fully accepting that I could lose Azaylia at any time.

You're telling me my daughter's got days to live? No. You're wrong.

Ashley was exactly the same and we were both defiantly keeping up the mantra that Azaylia was strong and she would beat the odds. She wasn't ready to go, not yet. That's what we said, because that's what we desperately needed to believe. If we didn't, how would we get through the next minute, let alone the next hour or the next day?

Making the moulds was one of the many ways we could distract ourselves with positivity. 'Isn't this beautiful?' I said to Azaylia. 'Your feet are so pretty. Look at those little toes! Look at your strong hands!' I wanted her to know that Mummy was there, watching out for her while she had her hands and feet dunked in this strange liquid. And most of all, I was determined to surround her with the same energy and love she had been used to all her life. She had to experience only happiness and love, it was the very least she deserved.

'I wanna be like you,' we sang to Azaylia when she opened her eyes and afterwards we posted a video on Instagram, showing the castings being made. It always gave me a boost to share special moments with our followers. *Here we are – still smiling! Still having fun! Still being brave!* The more we said it, the more believable it was. And we *had* to keep believing.

We also made prints of Azaylia's hands and feet, and we had three necklaces made, one for each of us. Azaylia's was in 24 carat gold – it had to be the purest gold we could get – and it had a heart on it, printed with mine, Ashley's and Azaylia's fingerprint.

I was on a mission to squeeze every drop of light and joy into my daughter's life and every day I wanted to be busy, busy, busy, though just getting myself out of bed was a monumental effort. I felt like I had chains holding me down on the mattress and my limbs were made of concrete.

'Good morning, beautiful princess!' I'd say to Azaylia, fear clawing at the back of my throat as I looked across at her. Ashley had given up his place in the bed so that Azaylia could sleep with me. 'How are you today?' Seeing her face always kicked the fear away, at least for a while.

I'd have loved it if all three of us could have shared the bed, but Azaylia's comfort had to come first and Ashley had volunteered to sleep on the settee downstairs. She needed plenty of space to lie comfortably on her back, and she was surrounded with her softest blankets and her favourite pillow.

Azaylia was no longer kicking her legs in excitement like she used to when she woke up in hospital, desperate to get up and play. She wasn't breaking into her trademark big smiles either but she was calm and settled and showing no signs of pain or discomfort, which was what mattered most. We had another precious day together and I was going to give her the best day I could.

Ashley had taken to staying up very late, listening to music and watching films on TV – anything to pass the time – and then he'd usually fall asleep on the settee in the early hours. I would have hated to be in a separate room to Azaylia, but the heartbreaking truth was that Ashley wasn't just making space for Azaylia in the bed. He was afraid we'd lose her in the night. He'd had nightmares about waking up in the morning and seeing his precious daughter's lifeless body, and so he preferred to stay downstairs.

Ashley barely slept – neither of us did – and in the morning, he'd come into our bedroom and be visibly overcome, flooded with relief that our daughter was still here.

'Come here, baby,' he'd say, kissing her and stroking her head. 'What shall we do today?'

She always rallied when she saw him, even if only in the tiniest way, and seeing the love that flowed between them never failed to bring tears to my eyes.

· · ·

The palliative care team came to the house. I knew this wasn't going to be easy, but I didn't expect my reaction to be so extreme. It was like death had walked in and a chill ran down my spine.

'Get out!' I wanted to scream. 'I don't want you in here!'

There were five members in the team and they all sat in a circle on our living-room floor, leaving me and Ashley and Azaylia to sit on the sofa. Azaylia was lying on a beanbag placed between us because that is where she seemed the most comfortable.

The nurses started to explain how they would help to make everything as comfortable as possible for Azaylia. I was nodding politely, though I felt like sticking my fingers in my ears and going 'la la la la la'. I didn't want to hear about end-of-life care. I wanted to keep my daughter alive and I was still going to care for her, monitor and protect her like I always had.

All the family came to visit, taking it in turns to hold Azaylia gently in their arms, or wrap their arms around the beanbag as she lay on it. They'd waited six months to hold her again, but of course their reunions were incredibly bittersweet. They knew we didn't want any sadness brought into the house and everyone was brilliant, trying to say only positive things and chatting about this, that and the other when they must have wanted to break down – I found it totally overwhelming.

Occasionally, when somebody did start to cry, I carried Azaylia quietly away from them and into another room. Everybody understood the situation and there was never any offence caused on either side. Ashley and me were so used to surrounding Azaylia with nothing but good energy. It was second nature to us, but of course we appreciated it wasn't like that for everyone. When the tears stopped, I'd bring Azaylia back in and we'd all start again.

My brother came with Noah. 'Let's have a photo!' I said, trying to keep the mood as light as possible. Noah stood next to Azaylia's ball pool on the floor and I held Azaylia protectively in my arms. I wanted to make a happy memory, but when I looked at Azaylia, I suddenly realised she didn't look like herself at all. She looked like a blank canvas.

'I want to reduce her pain relief,' I said. The palliative care nurses were guiding us all the way, but we were the ones nursing

Azaylia now and I was sure she would be better with a lower dose. I discussed this with the nurses, and they gave me the go-ahead, saying that we knew our daughter best and, as long as she was comfortable, it was fine by them.

I dialled down her Oramorph and guess what? Azaylia became herself again. She wasn't crying, she wasn't in discomfort and she was settled, most of the time. We could turn the dose up as and when she needed it.

Our daily routine was exhausting but, even if I could have rested, I wouldn't have done so. As long as I was doing *something* I was still being the best mummy I could to Azaylia.

• • •

I bought a shelf unit to use as a medicine station and installed it in the dining room. Every time we administered her meds they would be ticked off and recorded meticulously. The cleaning and sterilising of the house and all of Azaylia's things was still full-on, too. Even though Azaylia didn't need to be in a sterile environment any more, I never stopped scrubbing the floors and cleaning every surface – I didn't want her catching any kind of infection.

I was watching and listening for Azaylia's breathing all the time. Palliative care had been reluctant to give us the SATs machine, which monitors heart rate and other vital signs like oxygen levels and body temperature – 'Don't live off her SATs,' we were told – but I didn't want to hear it. I'd been in hospital with Azaylia long enough to know how to read her SATs, and if her heart rate was going sky-high, I wasn't going to sit back and do nothing. I was going to take her back to hospital and get it regulated.

Ashley's mum Vicky and his sister Alissia started staying over-night to help support us. I taught Vicky how to make up Azaylia's feeds and she did it perfectly, but I was very aware that I'd become the over-protective parent I never wanted to be, stand-ing over her shoulder and double-checking everything was being done correctly. I must have been so bossy and controlling, but Vicky understood how stressed and anxious I was and she offered nothing but unconditional love and support.

That's what being a mother is, I thought, watching her get on with things completely selflessly. I may have only been a mum for a very short time by comparison, but Azaylia had given me that gift: she had shown me how to love unconditionally.

. . .

'Shall we walk into town?' I said one morning, in a short window when all the jobs were done.

'Great idea,' Vicky said. 'It'll do us good.'

We put Azaylia in her pram, strolled into town and then sat on a bench and had a cup of coffee from Subway. Just for an hour, I was nothing but a proud mum, showing off my baby to the world and chatting with Ashley's mum about bits and bobs, nothing in particular. It was the same when my sister-in-law Michelle came and we took Noah to the swings. Azaylia loved watching her cousin playing and she was tracking him all the time as he swung back and forth, back and forth. *I wish one day we could be doing this too*, I thought.

This was how I imagined my life would be when I became a mother. Simple pleasures like this would fill my days. Now, any time spent with Azaylia and the family was so cherished and loaded with meaning. This was not going to last and this was not going to be my life. I was savouring every precious second and I was making a conscious effort to stay in the moment because that was the only way I could find any fragment of happiness. I managed it, mostly, though whatever way I looked, there was always an unwelcome reminder we were on borrowed time. It might be a glimpse from a stranger who did a double take at Azaylia's NG tube, wondering what was wrong with her. Or it could be an unfiltered, spontaneous thought that flashed across my mind but never made it to my lips: *When you're a big girl, Azaylia, you'll be able to play on the swings …*

Ashley's brother Matty and his girlfriend Amy brought Anaya over. The last time the two girls were in the same room together we were all blissfully unaware of what lay ahead. Seven months had passed since then and in all that time the girls had only seen each other through our front window.

Ashley wanted to take Azaylia outside in her pram to meet them and I got her dressed in a soft pink twinset and put her favourite pink bobble hat on her head so she was warm and cosy. I wanted Azaylia to properly meet her cousin, but I wasn't sure how I'd cope with the emotion of it all and the memories it would trigger. Amy and me had talked throughout our pregnancies about how lucky we were to both be having baby girls so close in age. When they were born six days apart we thought that was all that separated them. They'd start school together, we said. They'd learn how to ride their bikes together, and when they were older, we'd hoped the girls and Noah, and her other cousin Carmelo, would be as close as we were with all of our cousins on the Cain side of the family. It would be so tough to see them together today – those dreams were not going to come true and I didn't want to crumble.

Ashley was incredible. He carried Azaylia out to meet Anaya with a smile on his face and he made sure other members of the family took pictures of the moment the girls met, so we had a record. It was beautiful. The girls were both being held in their daddies' arms. Each spontaneously reached one arm out and gently touched hands. It's a moment Ashley said he would cherish forever.

'Are you doing OK?' I asked him.

'Yeah,' he said. 'It was such a happy, happy moment, even though it was filled with so much ...' He paused before adding one last word – 'sorrow.'

. . .

Azaylia's eyes had started to get puffy and they were gunky too, as if she had conjunctivitis. I cleaned them using sterilised water and I put cooling masks on her, using fresh gauzes that had been in the fridge. As soon as the masks reached room temperature, I swapped them over. It seemed to soothe her, but the gunk kept coming, so much so that her eyes were starting to close over.

One morning, both eyes were glued tight shut and no amount of gentle teasing and washing with sterilised water would open them. It was heartbreaking and I started to panic – it was as if she'd gone blind and I couldn't bear the thought.

What if she doesn't open her eyes again? What if she never sees Mummy or Daddy again?

I persevered with the sterilised gauzes and the cooling eye masks all day long until finally – bam! One eye popped open, then the other and she could see again. 'There you are!' I said, using a really calm voice that belied the avalanche of relief I was experiencing. I was so happy and proud of Azaylia. She wasn't in the dark any more, she wasn't giving up – of course she wasn't.

Ashley was still trying to be upbeat for Azaylia every single day but I could see behind his eyes how much he was struggling. Everybody who loved him could see how worried and upset he was but he carried on fighting with all his might, clutching at every positive he possibly could. He was singing to Azaylia now, like he did every day, and holding her gently in his arms as they danced together. There was no doubt Azaylia loved music and she never looked happier than when she was dancing in her daddy's arms. I loved to see it, but if Ashley had music on and Azaylia was in her car seat or on the beanbag, I didn't feel comfortable.

'Can you turn the music down?' I said, even though the volume was already low.

'Why? What's wrong?'

'I need to hear her breathing,' I explained.

Ashley nodded and turned the volume down. I was being over-anxious and hyper-vigilant, but of course he understood completely.

. . .

'Wanna hear something amazing, Azaylia?' I said one morning. 'Wanna know what's happening out there?' I was holding Azaylia in my arms at the front window, but there was nobody outside and nothing to see. 'I don't mean just here, on our road. I mean all over the big wide world, baby! You're an inspiration to so many people.'

Thousands of messages of love and support were still being posted online every day and lots of other wonderful things had started happening too.

'Listen to this, princess,' I said. 'This is for you, because you're such a special girl.'

London Underground's @allontheboard had put up a poem on their messageboard at North Greenwich station and I sat Azaylia in her car seat and read it all out to her: 'Sending love to Azaylia Cain, an 8-month-old beautiful little princess and a hero. Smiling despite being in discomfort and pain, fighting battles and shining like a diamond, providing light on the darkest of days; her determination and strength deserves everybody's love and respect in so many ways. No words can be written or spoken to fix hearts that are broken, all we can offer sometimes are thoughts, prayers and love; through the hardest and saddest times, Azaylia has shone brighter than any star up above.'

I had tears in my eyes. This was beautiful and it brought a much-needed ray of sunshine into our day. I could feel the light and love coming off that messageboard and straight into our home.

Later, after Azaylia had a long nap, I heard her stirring on her beanbag. 'Are you waking up, Azaylia?' I said, walking over to say hello. 'Let's see if Mummy needs to clean your pretty eyes, shall we?'

Taking care of Azaylia's eyes and keeping them cool if they looked sticky and swollen had become another one of my routine jobs. I knew the problem was caused by fluid retention in her body, which in turn was caused by her body shutting down. I'd managed to coax both of Azaylia's eyes open the first time they gummed up, but they were still looking very swollen and I was worried they'd stick together again in her sleep.

I bent over her beanbag and stopped in my tracks: the gunk in Azaylia's eyes was a much darker colour than before. I had a closer look. It wasn't just a darker colour, it was red. Blood red. And when Azaylia blinked, she had little red tears coming from her eyes.

Just before we left the hospital I managed to pluck up the courage to ask the end-of-life team how Azaylia would pass. I needed to know, so I could prepare myself as best I could, though it was the very last question I wanted to ask. The nurses had told me that when her body started shutting down it would produce fluid and that fluid wouldn't know where to go. It could make her eyes swollen to the point where they were sealed shut and there could be blood in her tears or in her nappy as the fluid escaped.

'Blood?' I'd said shakily. 'What do you mean, blood in her tears?'

There was no means of describing this in a way that was anything but deeply shocking and traumatising. When her organs were failing, Azaylia could start to bleed to death and the blood might come out of her eyes. I'd had to leave the room at that point because I was so distressed. How could my baby bleed to death from her eyes? How could Azaylia cry tears of blood? It was too horrific, too cruel. It was way too much to take on board and I shut it out of my head completely. I must have done a very good job of this because even when Azaylia's eyes had started to get sticky I still couldn't bring myself to return to that conversation.

Now I couldn't avoid it any longer. Every terrifying detail was crashing around my head and I could feel the panic rising.

'She's bleeding out!' I said to Ashley. 'She needs a platelet transfusion now!'

I knew full well by now that, when the blood of a leukaemia patient isn't clotting, they need more platelets. Nobody had told us to take Azaylia back to hospital if she bled from her eyes, but I wasn't waiting for a green light from anybody. This was an emergency and we needed to get our daughter to hospital ASAP. The hospital probably wouldn't like it because Azaylia was on end-of-life care but, if a transfusion was going to buy our baby more time, we were giving it to her – we *had* to give it to her.

We asked the nurses if we could drive Azaylia to hospital rather than calling an ambulance and they said yes, we could. We needed to take an oxygen cylinder with us. That was another fear I danced with every day: if Azaylia's oxygen levels dropped, she could die from having her brain starved of oxygen.

'Every day is a blessing,' I heard Ashley say as he carried Azaylia into the car. 'Azaylia is a beautiful little baby. She cannot bleed from the inside out. That is not the way my daughter is leaving this earth.'

CHAPTER
SEVENTEEN

'This is for you, princess. Look!'

Ashley was carrying Azaylia in his arms as we stepped outside the house. The amazing tributes and displays of support kept coming and now we had a plane drawing a heart and a letter 'A' in the sky.

'Wow! That's amazing!' I said, smiling and pointing at the sky. 'This is just for you, Azaylia!'

I'd never seen anything like this and it blew me away. The plane was cutting clear white lines through the bright blue sky, drawing the biggest heart in front of the cotton wool clouds. I wasn't expecting the letter 'A' to emerge too and it set my heart alight. Our family and neighbours came out of their houses to take a look and show support, people from other roads joined us too. Ashley and me both smiled and voiced our appreciation and we really did appreciate it, though behind our smiles we were falling apart.

Azaylia's platelet transfusion had stopped the tears of blood leaking from her eyes, but she still had fluid retention and swelling. Despite this I felt it was important to take her outside, even if only for a very brief amount of time. Me and Ashley had vowed to keep standing tall and strong. If there was a chance Azaylia could feel the love and support being showered on us from our community – and I'm certain she did – it was worth taking her outside. She could hear the clapping and I knew she loved that. As Ashley said, we were making the days count, not counting the days.

After the display we closed the front door behind us and were straight back into medical mode, filling syringes and preparing to give Azaylia her next lot of medication. Our home had become a makeshift hospital. Azaylia's life was ebbing away, there was no denying that. Part of me wanted to close the blinds, switch off my phone and shut out the world. We could be in our little family bubble and Ashley and me would take it from here and do all of this on our own. Of course, I knew before the thought had finished crossing my mind that it wasn't the right thing to do. We needed the family support we had in our home and sharing our story had brought us so much love and support.

I picked up my phone and composed a post to my Instagram followers, telling them all about the airplane display and sharing a video. I wasn't just being brave or forcing myself to do the right thing, I found it therapeutic to share my feelings on social media and in any case, I wasn't just talking to my followers, I was talking to Azaylia too. I hadn't ever made a conscious decision to address her directly, it had just happened, very naturally.

'I'm so proud of you, Azaylia, you're beautiful,' I wrote online. 'I'm so blessed to have another day with you. I have never felt so scared, nervous and anxious in my life, my heart aches heavy all through the day but being able to love and care for you is the biggest gift of my life. Your battle against AML [acute myeloid leukaemia] has inspired so many people to show kindness. This is so beautiful to see. You are bringing everyone together. Thank you for all the beauty & lighting up the world for my little girl.'

Replies started to pour in straight away. 'I find it so difficult watching your videos, it is heartbreaking to see Azaylia so poorly,' one follower wrote. 'You are doing your little lion so proud every single day.'

Another said: 'You're such an amazing family. Azaylia is so lucky to have such a supportive family behind her.'

All this warmth and love was balm to my soul and social media never stopped surprising us with gift after gift.

Actor and former professional wrestler Dwayne 'The Rock' Johnson posted a video on Instagram, telling Ashley how sorry he was to hear Azaylia's prognosis. 'I don't have to tell you,' he said, 'that your daughter's strength is what strengthens you and all her loved ones around her. And in that, she has already had this incredible impact on the world. Stay strong, brother, man my heart breaks for you, and tell that little lion, I said: "Let's go, champ".'

Ashley's a huge fan of The Rock and he felt so moved and humbled by his words. The support we were getting from all round the world was absolutely phenomenal.

●　●　●

We didn't know our followers personally, but it didn't feel like that. They had become like family and whenever I looked on my Instagram I felt protected by them. It was like having thousands of pillows to lean into.

The last comment I read that day simply said: 'Such a brave and beautiful little girl who has won our hearts.' That said it all. My little girl had won hearts all over the planet and that was a testament to her amazing personality and her fighting spirit. What an absolutely amazing achievement and what a lesson she was to us all.

We'd been at home for nine days when our followers came up trumps again, organising a national clap for Azaylia at 7pm one evening. As soon as I heard about it, I went online, asking people to record themselves on their doorsteps and post their videos to an email address we had set up.

I wanted to see all the love and share as much of it as I could with Azaylia, but she was really struggling that day. She'd lost some movement in her face because of the fluid building up inside her and little bruises were appearing on her body. I was in two minds whether to take her outside, but she was calm and seemed comfortable when it was finally time to make the decision.

I got her dressed in cosy clothes, made sure she was snug in her pink bobble hat and went out to join in, holding Azaylia in my arms. All our neighbours were out, and when the clapping started, me and Ashley did what we'd got used to doing. We put on a brave face, we let people take photos, we made sure we said thank you and we made our own videos. All the while we told Azaylia what was happening, in her name.

'Well done, baby,' I told her. 'This is because you are so brave and strong and we all love you so much.'

So many emotions were swirling around me. I was humbled and buoyed by the clap. It cost nothing, it took just a few minutes and yet it meant so much. I felt so grateful to our followers for organising it and to all the people who joined in but my heart was breaking. We should have been inside doing normal family stuff instead of clapping on our doorstep for our daughter. This wasn't meant to be our life. Azaylia should have been going to bed after having her night-time bath and me and Ashley should be cuddled up on the settee, chilling out and enjoying being new parents.

• • •

Later that same evening, after the clapping event, I was shocked to see Azaylia had a large purple mark on the inside of her right thigh. I saw it when I went to change her, and it was more than a bruise.

'She needs another platelet transfusion,' I said, without hesitation, because I knew that if she had normal levels of platelets in her blood it would have clotted instead of bleeding into the skin like this.

When we checked her heart rate it was racing at over 200 beats per minute so we called an ambulance and took her straight in to hospital again that night. There was absolutely nothing to discuss. Once again, it was a case of: 'If Azaylia needs platelets, Azaylia is having platelets.'

The doctors and nurses who took care of her were amazingly helpful and efficient. They got her temperature and heart rate down, checked her for infections and gave her another small plate-let transfusion. We were incredibly grateful. To have a hospital like Birmingham on our doorstep was an absolute blessing and we thanked our lucky stars. The swelling in Azaylia's eyes went down quite noticeably and she quickly looked brighter and more like herself. It was such a relief. Azaylia had really pushed the boundar-ies. The doctors had not expected her to live this long, but she was still here and still in our arms. The NHS had just gifted us a little bit more time and we would never be able to repay them for that.

'Mummy and Daddy promised to give you 100 per cent from day one, didn't we, baby?' I said to Azaylia when we were travel-ling home. 'We're keeping to our word and whatever you need, we will provide for you, baby.'

Later that night I updated my followers, explaining that we'd had to take Azaylia to hospital after the clapping. She was so much better now and I sat her on my lap and sang Mariah Carey's 'Miracle' to her before finally taking a look at some of the videos people had sent in.

I was completely unprepared for the scale of the event. Thou-sands and thousands of people took part in the clap, from all around the world. Mrs Hinch and Marnie Simpson from *Geordie Shore* joined in. Abbey Clancy and Peter Crouch filmed their kids on their doorstep, and reality star Stacey Solomon sent a beau-tiful message of support because she couldn't make it home in time. I was blown away.

'You're an inspiration, baby,' Ashley said to Azaylia a few days later. 'Everyone is so proud of you. You're literally lighting up the world!'

Before our daughter became ill, I had no idea that leukaemia awareness is represented by the colour orange. I didn't know how it started, but landmarks around the UK had been lighting up orange, in support of Azaylia and leukaemia awareness. First, it was Clacton Pier and Liverpool's Radio City Tower, and one by one, we watched as Wembley Stadium, Newcastle's Millennium Bridge, Nuneaton Town Hall, Coventry's Whittle Arch, Blackpool Tower and the London Eye all lit up orange. It was absolutely mind-blowing. So many monuments joined in, I was finding it hard to keep track and Azaylia's story was being shared by millions of people and news organisations across the world.

'What's going on now?' I asked.

'You're not gonna believe it!' Ashley replied, and he was right.

Landmarks overseas were starting to join in with the support. Toronto's CN Tower turned a spectacular bright orange, and now Ashley was telling me that Niagara Falls had followed suit.

'Niagara Falls?' I repeated. 'Are you serious?'

I watched the images in awe, mesmerised by the sight of thousands of tons of crashing water lighting up in the most vibrant shade of orange. It was such a powerful and poignant statement and seeing those pictures for the first time is something I will never forget.

Azaylia was in my arms as I drank in the magnitude of the display and what it represented. She was a precious, delicate little girl, but somehow she had roared like a lioness, turned a gigantic, world-famous waterfall orange and made her story heard right across the globe.

'Look what you've done, Azaylia!' I said to her. 'Everyone is so proud of you! You've made all that water turn orange. YOU did that, Azaylia. You're so magical, it's amazing.'

Ashley and me had always said we wanted our daughter to grow up knowing the world was her oyster. She could do anything she wanted in life, be anyone she wanted to be and make her mark on the world in whatever way she saw fit. Azaylia had achieved a dazzling amount in her short life. She was absolutely incredible and I was bursting with pride.

. . .

As usual, after the rainbow came another storm. While the landmarks were lighting up orange in the middle of April 2021, Azaylia was bleeding from her eyes again and she was having nosebleeds too. We took her back to hospital for a third time and got her checked over and given platelets.

We were at the front of the hospital, on our way back to the car, when I suddenly felt her go heavy in my arms: 'Ashley, get the oxygen!' I screamed. Azaylia's eyes were rolling back in her head, she felt very hot and she wasn't breathing. There was no time to take her back inside the hospital and Ashley shot off at breakneck speed to fetch the oxygen tank from our car. 'Hurry up, get it now!' I screamed after him.

Within minutes, we managed to bring Azaylia back round. God knows what anyone would have thought if they saw us giving our collapsed daughter oxygen in the grounds of Birmingham Children's Hospital, but we had to act quickly. If we'd wasted precious minutes carrying Azaylia back inside and asking for help, it could have been too late.

It was a massive relief to get her home. She had cooled down and looked much more comfortable now, but later that night the same thing started happening all over again. Her temperature spiked and she looked like she was having a seizure in her cot. This time, after bringing her round once more with oxygen, we called out a nurse from the palliative care team to check her over.

It was the early hours by the time Azaylia was stable and settled and we finally got to bed. I couldn't sleep a wink and I watched Azaylia breathing deep into the night.

We were doing what we promised Azaylia we would do, I thought. We were giving 100 per cent and matching her in courage and tenacity, all the way. Her pain relief was being managed and, as long as she was not suffering, we would keep fighting for every last second with her.

I was watching Azaylia intently when she woke up early in the morning.

'Hello, princess,' I said as she prised her little eyes open, ever so slowly. My baby was still here and she smiled at me. It was the softest, most gentle little smile in the world and it made my heart flutter. It was just the sign I needed. Azaylia knew we were fighting with all our might for her and I would keep on fighting, just as hard as she was.

.   .   .

A nurse from the palliative care team suggested we should start reducing the amount of food we gave to Azaylia, explaining that her body would no longer be able to digest it as she came to the end of her life.

'No,' I said. 'She needs her food. She needs to get strong.'

Azaylia would start to pass white poo eventually, we were told. This was because her digestive system was failing and the milk would go straight through her. That was another sign that she was reaching the end of her life and we should prepare for it.

There was no way I was going to deny my baby any of her food. I knew Azaylia wasn't going to get strong. I accepted that in my head, but my heart was raging against this advice. Even if we only got another day with Azaylia, we had to try our hardest to keep her here.

Ashley's mum Vicky cooked us some lunch one day and I managed to feed some solid food to Azaylia. Surprisingly, it was a green bean that she took a shine to and she chomped on it and waved it around happily.

'Clever girl, eating your greens!' I said.

Azaylia was not just alive, she was still making the most of every day. She was absolutely remarkable.

CHAPTER
EIGHTEEN

The nurses came early in the morning, for a routine home visit. 'Enjoy this weekend,' they said, giving kind and sympathetic smiles. 'You should make the most of it.'

I felt a cold wind blow through my bones. We'd had Azaylia at home for more than two weeks now, despite the much darker prognosis we'd been given when she was discharged from hospital, but her body was shutting down now, there was no getting away from that. She had been moved from Oramorph onto a stronger type of morphine and it was too late to call out ambulances any more.

This isn't happening! This can't be happening! There was a voice in my head screaming and protesting, but who was going to listen? Nobody was listening, because there was nothing that could be done. Azaylia looked more tired than she ever had. Our daughter was in charge now and we had to listen to *her*, however painful it was to accept what was unfolding.

I wheeled Azaylia outside in her pram, so she could get some fresh air and listen to some different sounds. They were simple pleasures, but it's the small things in life that make a difference. That's what I thought as I stood beside her, breathing in the April breeze and holding my beautiful daughter's hand. She lifted her other arm and put it over her face. She was worn out, bless her – I'd never seen her look so spent and exhausted.

That night, Ashley came to sleep in our bed instead of on the settee. I sang 'When You Believe' to our daughter as I got her ready for bed. 'This is one of our songs,' I told her. 'It will always remind me of you.'

We laid Azaylia very carefully between us because we wanted her to feel that comfort of having Mummy and Daddy around her and she drifted quietly off to sleep. As usual I lay there listening to her breathing, but it was harder than ever to keep myself from falling apart. I felt sick to my stomach and worried out of my mind. How can you feel anything different when you know the life is gradually leaving your daughter's body and she's lying right there beside you? Ashley and me took it in turns to close our eyes, but we only snatched minutes of sleep, when our bodies forced us to accept it.

When I opened my eyes, it was finally morning, Azaylia was just waking up too. It was 24 April 2021 and I took one look at her and I knew, instinctively, that this was the day. She was pale and had a very vulnerable look about her, one I hadn't seen before. Ashley had always been so scared of her passing in the night, slipping away when we were asleep. Maybe Azaylia knew that, I thought. Maybe that's why she was still here, waiting for daylight, sparing her daddy and me an extra coat of grief we didn't want to wear.

Numbness descended on me. I got up and went downstairs. Vicky and Alissia had stayed over and I told them: 'This is it, this is the day.'

When I walked back into the bedroom, Ashley and me gave each other a knowing look, acknowledging what was happening. Azaylia's breathing had become very slow and shallow. Ashley gently moved her to the end of the bed while I got the SATs machine and tried to attach it to her toe, to monitor her heart rate. It wouldn't pick up her pulse the way it normally did so I took it off and tried to re-attach it. I was struggling and starting to panic – why wasn't this machine working? What was wrong with it?

I lifted the tab off Azaylia's toe and put it to the side, finally accepting it was no longer of any use. Ashley was lying alongside Azaylia now and I was kneeling on the floor in front of her. The urge to scoop my daughter into my arms was incredibly power-ful, but I didn't do it. The tumours in Azaylia's little body had been getting bigger. We'd been handling her like a delicate flower and I was terrified that if I lifted her now I might press on her stomach and hurt her, or dislodge something. That was the very last thing I wanted to do.

The gaps between Azaylia's breaths were getting a little longer every time. I asked Alissia to call my brother, because his house is fifteen minutes away. I wanted Danny here. He'd been with me on this whole journey and he was my best friend and my rock.

Azaylia hung on until my brother arrived. Her eyes were shut tight, but I'm sure she knew what was happening. I felt she could still see all of us, in a way.

The palliative care team arrived and Vicky, Alissia and Danny gathered in the bedroom to support us.

When Azaylia's breaths finally stopped coming, Ashley and me lay either side of her on the bed, wrapping our arms around her ever so gently. 'We love you,' we told her. 'We love you, Azaylia.'

From the moment she passed, Azaylia looked incredibly peaceful. It was as if her last breath blew out all the discomfort she had in her body and she was immediately rested.

I was crying but I was also in a drone-like state, as if my mind and body had decided I couldn't cope with anything else, not yet. There was too much to process. It was very quiet in the room, *too* quiet. Then Ashley suddenly started shaking all over, his limbs jolting everywhere.

I was looking round the room and calling for help: 'What's wrong? Someone help!'

It was like he was having a fit. His body had seized up and he was no longer in control of himself.

The palliative care nurses came rushing over. I heard one of them yelling for gas and air, which shot a memory across my mind: *Gas and air! I need it, NOW PLEASE!* I picked Azaylia up and I went and sat with her on the top stair. Her body had passed now, but her soul and her energy were still around. Our daughter had never experienced shouting voices and I didn't want her exposed to any chaos or raised voices now.

'It'll be OK in a minute,' I told her, rocking her in my arms. 'You know Daddy. Silly Daddy, what's he doing?'

Ashley came round quickly. We didn't discuss what had happened. He was clearly in shock but he was OK now, and it was a case of 'what's next? What do we do now?'

In the last couple of weeks the palliative care team had talked to us about preparing the clothes we wanted to put Azaylia in immediately after she passed, along with plenty of other things I didn't take on board. While she was still alive, I didn't want to spend time organising clothes to lay my daughter to rest in – I preferred to spend my time with her, in the here and now.

'Did you choose an outfit? Do you want to get her clean?'

The nurses were lovely, wanting to make sure we did exactly what we wanted to do with Azaylia in these important minutes. I'd just have to take one step at a time and work my way through whatever needed to happen next.

'Azaylia loved a bath,' I said. 'Yes, I want to give her a bath.'

Ashley and me bathed her together. It was far too quiet in the bathroom. I used to do crazy Mummy dancing at bath-time, singing along to Disney music or Whitney Houston, but now there was only the sound of slowly moving water and mine and Ashley's voices, talking to her softly.

I looked at Azaylia's little body. My daughter had turned into a porcelain doll. She'd had hundreds of baths in hospital and she loved every one. Even when she was so poorly and sick, Azaylia splashed and she played in the bubbles, making the very best of it.

'Here you go,' Azaylia, I soothed, wiping her little face. 'This will make you all clean and fresh.'

Ashley was very quiet. We were in this together, experiencing the same painful emotions, and there were no words we could use that would make this situation any easier.

I fetched some oil to put on Azaylia's skin and after we'd washed and dried her, we rubbed it gently all over her body. She wasn't in any pain now. That's what I told myself, again and again. She was so comfortable, so peaceful.

I put her usual cream on too and I put her in a fresh nappy. Then I dressed her in a vestgro and her Lion King printed jump-suit, one she'd worn so many times before. It smelled of Fairy washing powder, like it always did.

'Where's her hat?' I said.

Someone passed it to me. It was her favourite pink woollen hat with the pom-pom on top, the one I always put her in when-ever we were outside. I wanted her to wear it now because I could feel her body going cold.

'There you go, Azaylia,' I told her. 'This will keep you warm.'

I asked the nurses to remove her NG tube – 'Please, take it all off her. All the stickers, let her be comfortable now.' They did what they could, but her central line was still in place. I didn't like it there, but they couldn't remove it easily and it had to stay, at least for now.

When Azaylia was all fresh and ready, we invited other close family members to the house to say goodbye. Ashley put Azay-lia's music on in the living room and everyone took his or her turn holding her, or having a little dance with her. 'I Wanna Be Like You' was Azaylia's all-time favourite, and everyone wanted to hear it. It was so apt, I thought. *Who wouldn't want to be like you, Azaylia?*

People who held her cried their eyes out. It was utterly heart-breaking to see. I felt numb with shock and panic and I was crying. I still felt Azaylia's presence so powerfully, all around me. Me and Ashley stayed close to whoever was holding our daughter. We both found it difficult to be away from her, because every minute was so precious.

Later that morning, Azaylia was taken to the funeral parlour. We were using Devalls, which was run by a family friend, and Ashley travelled with Azaylia while me and my brother followed behind in my car, bringing lots of her toys and belongings with us. Danny was brilliant. I was leaning on him heavily and he was soaking up so much of my pain and offering me endless support.

I was frightened of what it would be like at the funeral home, but when I saw Azaylia lying in her own little room, in a cot, she looked at peace and she looked cosy. I still felt scared, but I also relaxed slightly. That was more than I could have hoped for. It was explained to me that I could visit however often I wanted during their opening hours of 8.30am to 5pm and they would always bring her out into this room, ready for me to see her.

'Thank you,' I said, relief washing through me.

I hadn't ever allowed my head to go to a place like this, but I felt reassured now I'd seen it. It wasn't scary here; it was tranquil and calm, and it felt like a safe place for Azaylia to rest.

'Here you are, princess,' I said, peering into her cot. 'I brought all of your things.'

I laid Simba and Nala beside her and a few of her favourite rattles and toys. I brought a soft blanket too and I snuggled that around her.

'Look who else I brought,' I said. 'It's the angel!'

Whenever Azaylia was going for a procedure in hospital, or changing wards, I used to tell her that we had three wishes with this angel. We would always wish for things like good health, for Azaylia to be able to go home soon, or for her next surgery or treatment to be successful. Sometimes we wished for fun things, like making sandcastles or splashing in the sea instead of just sitting in a plastic NHS bathtub. I placed the little angel beside her.

'I know she turned out to be a rubbish angel,' I said, 'but you liked her, didn't you? So here she is. She's going to lie here with you.'

· · ·

I visited Azaylia in the Chapel of Rest every day, usually more than once. I read books to her for hours on end and I took different toys in, rotating them so she always had something different. Azaylia's spirit was still here, I could feel it, and so I wanted to keep surrounding her with good energy and love.

Going to the chapel gave my life purpose and it stopped me from breaking. I couldn't take grief and fear into my baby's room and so time spent with her was respite from the darkness that enveloped me at home, or when I was driving my car.

Every morning when I woke up and remembered all over again that Azaylia had passed, I didn't want to live. What was the point of living? I was nothing and nobody any more. My dreams of motherhood had been shattered, my future taken away from me. Seeing her things all around the house was unbearable. All the thoughts I'd had about Azaylia growing up and the girl and woman she would become had been extinguished.

I found it so hard to lift myself out of bed. The chains were back, pulling me into the mattress, and even when I'd managed to get to my feet, I felt shackled everywhere. My concrete legs were back with a vengeance; I felt like I couldn't even walk.

Sharing the news of Azaylia's passing with our followers was so hard, but it was something we had to do. 'You are my angel, my heartbeat, my soul,' I wrote. 'RIP my precious baby, you will always be with me, like a handprint on my heart.'

Ashley said: 'Rest in paradise princess. I will always hold you in my heart until I can hold you again in heaven.'

We'd never really talked about heaven, but I shared Ashley's view, 100 per cent. Heaven existed and we would meet our daughter again one day, if we earned our place there. That was the only thing that kept the darkest thoughts out of my head. When I was driving in my car, I didn't care if I crashed. Sometimes I thought about just doing it, because then my daily torture would end and I wouldn't have to live this pointless half-life any more. Because without Azaylia, that's what my life was: it was a life with no purpose, no hope. When I thought about the future there was nothing there. It was an empty, black void. But I couldn't take my own life, could I? My daughter had fought so hard for hers and she would not have wanted me to cut mine short. She would want me to fight and be brave, just like her, and I wasn't going to let her down.

The idea of heaven, and being reunited with Azaylia, was a huge motivator. To get to heaven I had to be a better person, and I had to inspire others, just like Azaylia did. I would do my very best, however much I wanted to close my eyes and never open them again. Ashley helped me a lot. He said he totally understood how I felt as he felt the same way, and he always reminded me that we needed to stay here on earth and make Azaylia proud in order to earn our place with her.

Our charity idea was on ice for now. There was no way we could give it any of the attention it needed, but whenever I thought about creating a legacy for Azaylia, the future wasn't a big black hole any more. I could see some purpose and some hope, a flicker of light at the end of the longest tunnel. If I could just keep putting one foot in front of the other, eventually I'd find daylight again. The sun would be out and I'd carry on, walking tall in Azaylia's shadow, carrying her gifts forward.

CHAPTER
NINETEEN

'Saf, come and look at this!'

Ashley's face was alight. It was the first time I'd seen him smile since Azaylia passed. When I stepped out of our front door I couldn't believe what I was seeing. I gasped and a big smile stretched across my face too. It was dusk and the most vibrant orange sunset had spilled into the giant swirling clouds, lighting up the whole sky to the left of our house.

'It's Azaylia!' I said. 'Hello, beautiful girl!'

Every day, when I drove to and from the Chapel of Rest, I asked for signs from Azaylia. I still felt her presence very strongly. Her soul and her energy were still around us on earth, I felt sure of that. I looked for a sign that she could still see Mummy and Daddy, wherever she was on her journey to heaven.

Show me you can see me. Show me you are there, Azaylia.

And now here she was, in all her magnificent glory.

'Only Azaylia could do this,' I said. 'I didn't expect the sign to be this big, but of course it would be! She's one in a million!'

'And the rest!' Ashley said, laughing as he looked high into the sky. 'You're one in a trillion, million, billion, aren't you, baby?'

Azaylia had filled us with so much belief when she was with us and it was truly breathtaking that she was still doing it from the heavens. We both blew kisses up into the clouds, told her how much we missed her and asked her to keep bringing us signs, as many as she could, as often as she liked.

'I don't know how you do it, Azaylia,' Ashley said. 'But please keep doing it! Keep making us believe, princess.'

• • •

It was time to start making plans to lay Azaylia to rest. I was very unsure and nervous about it and, at first, I didn't even want my brain to go there. I told Ashley I just wanted it to be a low-key and intimate occasion. I'd wear a tracksuit and a hoodie, because that's how I'd been living in hospital for so long.

But Ashley had been thinking and he didn't agree. 'Azaylia's gonna be watching us,' he said, 'and she's been watching us in hoodies and being scruffy for so long in hospital. Let's show her some respect? Let's get dressed properly and be smart and make her proud of us?'

He was making a very good point and, for the first time, I was ready to listen and think about the day.

'We want Azaylia to say, "Look at Mummy and Daddy coming to my day,"' he went on. '"Look at how clean and smart they are.

Mummy's hair's all done, they've got fresh clothes and shoes on." I want to be able to tell her: "This is for you, Azaylia. We've made this day as beautiful and special as you. It's what you deserve.'"

Ashley was absolutely right and I was sold, 100 per cent.

After we'd discussed a few ideas between ourselves, we went to the funeral directors and shared them with Danny Devall, who would be in charge of all the organisation. I told Danny I wanted to call it Azaylia's Day. The usual word for the occasion just didn't sit right – it made me think of death when I wanted to think of light. Azaylia was a beacon of hope and an inspiration. I wanted the day we laid her to rest to be a celebration of how brightly she shone.

We'd thought about wearing white to reflect Azaylia's purity and innocence, but Ashley came up with a really lovely idea: if we had white horses around the carriage, and Azaylia was laid in a white casket, we should wear black. That way we were blacked out and she was the light – the star of the show. I loved that idea. We would wear orange accessories to show our support for leukaemia awareness. It was slowly starting to come together and at last I was starting to allow myself to plan and prepare.

Azaylia would be in the Chapel of Rest for several weeks because of delays caused by the pandemic and we were warned that, after the first week, her appearance would probably start to change. Ashley chose not to keep visiting every day and I totally respected his decision. Quite rightly, he said goodbye to Azaylia when the time felt right to him and he would be with her again on Azaylia's Day.

I felt very differently, continuing to visit Azaylia two or three times every day. I wanted to make the most of still being able to give her a kiss or hold her hand, and I wanted to check up on her, to make sure she was being well looked after. I knew she was, but I wanted to see for myself, like mums do.

I was given an embalming paste to put on Azaylia's nose and her lips and her fingers and toes, because babies don't have their bodies embalmed, they are left in a natural state. I would put the cream on her once or twice a day, to stop her skin wrinkling and drying out, and it worked. She still looked beautiful and plump-cheeked every single day.

I always busied myself with organising her toys and rotating them, taking comfort from the fact I could still be a hands-on mum, doing practical things for my baby.

'I've brought you these butterflies,' I told her one day. 'Aren't they pretty?'

I arranged the silver and pink paper butterflies all around her cot to bring beauty to her surroundings. They were one of the many gifts we'd received since Azaylia passed. Thoughtful presents arrived from our followers every day and our living room was filling up with the most beautiful personalised keepsakes, photos, candles and pieces of art. People sent poems too and I'd read them to her, as well as pages from her nursery rhyme or Disney books – 'Which one d'you want next, princess? Shall we read your *CoComelon* book today?'

Every time I drove home I looked up at the sky for signs Azaylia was there, watching. And she was, all the time. It was incredible.

Never in my life had I seen so many dramatic sunsets and swirling orange clouds. They followed me around, always filling me with joy. Often I was at home as the sun started to set and I got used to opening the front door, looking to the left and waiting to see what orange masterpiece Azaylia had drawn for me today.

. . .

When Azaylia was in hospital I used to dream about the day she had her central line taken out. It was still attached to her – she had two now, one on either side of her chest – and it bothered me. I didn't want Azaylia to be rested with tubes in her body. I wanted her to be pure, without any reminders of all the medical interventions she had been through.

I asked the palliative care team if they could help and two nurses agreed to come to the Chapel of Rest.

'I want to be in the room when you do it,' I said.

'Are you sure?'

They warned me that though Azaylia's beautiful little face hadn't altered – she still had peaches in her cheeks – her body might have changed colour.

'I understand,' I said. 'But I'll stay.'

I was with Azaylia every time she was put to sleep in hospital and I wanted to be with her for this.

I sat on a chair while the nurses gently undressed Azaylia and started to remove the lines. It was a struggle for them and there was some blood. My eyes flicked to Azaylia's stomach and I saw that her skin had turned a greeny colour. I looked past it straight away, turning my gaze on her face and fixating on her beautiful features. Her face still looked cherubic, like an angel – I didn't take my eyes off it until the job was done.

I took the lines and put them in a special box I had. I wasn't sure what I was going to do with them, I just knew I wanted to keep them.

The nurses cleaned away the blood and asked if I wanted to change Azaylia into a different outfit. The thought of it frightened me. I didn't know how Azaylia's body would move. She was cold now and I was afraid I might break her little arm or dislodge something.

I had thought about putting her in a pretty dress and some tights, but that wasn't Azaylia. She was always jamming in her onesies, her vests and her socks. I wanted her to be comfortable and I told the nurses I wanted to put her back in her lion outfit she had been dressed in since we bathed her at home. She looked so peaceful and rested, I didn't want to cause any distress to her body by moving her around.

The nurses helped me as I carefully dressed Azaylia back in the lion suit. I changed her socks, putting her in a bright orange pair, and I put her favourite fluffy pink bobble hat on so she wasn't cold. I always loved her in that hat – she looked like a pretty ray of sunshine.

• • •

On the day Azaylia turned nine months I was going to have my hair done for the first time in ages, by my friend in her salon. I felt really guilty about it. How could I have time for myself when I could be sitting with Azaylia? My friend wouldn't hear it: she knew that when I wasn't with Azaylia I didn't know what to do with myself and I often sat in bed and cried.

'A bit of pampering will do you good,' she said. 'And you have absolutely nothing to feel guilty about.'

I visited Azaylia in the morning and told her all about it.

'Will you come and sit with me?' I asked.

I was sure that she would.

My friend was opening her salon just for me, because she knew I was struggling and she wanted to give me some privacy. As soon as I walked in the door 'Angel of Mine' by Eternal came on the radio. I often played that song in my car and I'd sung it to Azaylia so many times recently. It's a song that can't fail to pull at your heartstrings, taking about perfect love and what it means. It had become an anthem to me and hearing it now brought me peace. It told me that Azaylia had come with me, just like I asked her to. It was OK to be here – I had her blessing and she was sitting with me.

We were lighting a candle that night, to mark Azaylia's nine months, and on the way home I did what I always did, looking for a sign in the sky that Azaylia was watching.

I'd bought a new pair of Simba and Nala teddies because we'd decided that when we closed Azaylia's casket we would take out her old ones and replace them, so we could keep the originals.

'I've got Simba and Nala with me in the car, because I'm sitting them next to the candle tonight, princess,' I said, scanning the clouds. 'They will be watching when we celebrate your nine months. Are you watching me now, Azaylia?'

To my astonishment, the most beautiful rainbow appeared in the sky, right on cue. I hadn't seen a rainbow in years. I got goose-bumps all down my arms and I tingled with happiness.

'Thank you, Azaylia,' I said, starting to cry. 'You're so clever, magnifying your energy like this! Can you hear Mummy, baby? I love you.'

'After the storm comes a rainbow' was a phrase I heard the nurses use many times in hospital, but I could never identify with it.

Where's the rainbow? Where is it?

When I was looking for rainbows they didn't come, but guess what? Now they were popping up without us even asking for them.

Ashley FaceTimed me when I was in the car with his mum one day to say there was the most beautiful rainbow in the sky and to get home quick so I could see it from our house. I wasn't far away and when I looked in my rear-view mirror I could see it behind us. I told Ashley's mum Vicky we'd have to pull over – it was absolutely magnificent and I didn't want to miss a single moment of it. A few days later, a double rainbow lit up the sky. It was pulsating with light and colour, so vibrant I felt I could reach out and touch it. I'd never even seen a double rainbow before and this one was an absolute stunner, painted right in front of the house, just for us.

'Wow, Azaylia!' I said. 'That's so beautiful! Look at what you're doing, lighting the sky back up for us.'

Azaylia's presence was dazzling us, every single day. It reached the point where I'd walk out of my front door and didn't know which way to look first. If I looked to the left, would Azaylia have waved her magic wand and turned the blue sky to orange? If I looked to the right, would today be a day when she drew electric rainbows to brighten our day? Ashley spotted a letter 'A' written in amongst some orange clouds one day and we saw the shape of a little lion head that looked just like Nala and Simba.

'Azaylia, you are AMAZING!' I told her, gazing into the heavens. 'You are an absolute STAR!'

•   •   •

All the preparations for Azaylia's Day were coming together. Danny Devall had been absolutely fantastic – he had a great team helping him and every last detail had been thought through. We would give Azaylia a day that matched her in style and spirit and strength and positivity. I was in no doubt about that; it would be an incredibly special celebration of her life.

We'd all worked hard and I was proud of everything we'd put in place, but as the day drew closer, waves of dread were crashing in. I'd got used to my routine of visiting Azaylia whenever I wanted in her room at the Chapel of Rest and now everything would change. I didn't want to think about what lay ahead and I worried that my little girl would be lonely or afraid when I didn't visit her every day.

I bought a toy mobile phone and placed it beside her in her cot. 'You can take this to heaven with you,' I said. 'And then you can always call me, any time you want. I'll always be here for you.'

Two days before Azaylia's Day, I was sitting with Ashley on the grass in front of our house, both of us in total awe of the sight before us. The whole sky had turned the brightest, most vibrant orange. Pulsing with colour, it kept on getting brighter and brighter. It was like the whole sky was on fire, as far as the eye could see, and then – bam! – a heart-shaped gap appeared in the clouds. We drank in the scene, devouring every moment. Azaylia had done *all* of this for us. Her strength and courage were shining down from the sky, soothing and bolstering our hearts.

The sky was so dramatic that night it made the local news, with reporters describing it as a 'fire sky'. In our eyes this was no quirk of nature or natural phenomenon – it was all Azaylia's doing, no question about it. Ashley shared pictures with his followers.

'There's no such thing as good and bad days at the moment,' he wrote. 'There's bad and worse. But after another painful day, asking and praying for Azaylia to give me a sign that she's OK … this happened tonight!' He described the cloud and said Azaylia had peeped through the gap so we could see her beautiful face. 'I couldn't have wished for a more magical evening and through so much pain, she's still bringing me the glimpses of happiness that I need! I cry so much at the moment … But tonight, baby, tonight I smile! I LOVE YOU, CHAMP.'

• • •

Though Ashley had already said goodbye to Azaylia at the Chapel of Rest, he came with me when it was finally time to place her in her casket. We had both decided to write a letter to our daughter to put inside the casket with her. Mine was done and Ashley was sitting outside in the reception area, putting the finishing touches to his.

Knots tightened in my stomach when Danny brought the tiny white casket into Azaylia's room. We'd taken a lot of time choosing the style and deciding how to decorate it, with diamond jewels all around the edges, but it was still a shock to see it in front of me.

'Wow,' I said to Danny. 'It looks beautiful. It looks so pure.'

The inside was lined with silk and I reached in and touched it. It was so fine and soft, and that brought me some comfort – that's what I wanted for Azaylia's forever home. There was orange piping around the edge of the inside of the casket and the words 'Oh, oobee doo, I wanna be like you' were embroidered on top of the casket, in orange stitching. We *did* want to be like Azaylia. She was so strong and brave; she was an example to Ashley and me, and to the thousands of other people she had inspired.

I'd already agreed with Danny that I was going to pick Azaylia up and lay her in the casket, but when the moment came I started trembling and crying uncontrollably. I hadn't held my baby in my arms for weeks and weeks. I desperately wanted to hold her, but knowing it would be the very last time was devastating and I was really struggling to stop my tears.

Danny offered to do it for me. 'No,' I said, thanking him. All the while I was thinking, *I'm Azaylia's mum, nobody else can do this*. Somehow I composed myself and lifted Azaylia out of the Moses basket she was lying in and into my arms. I was incredibly nervous, not knowing how her limbs or her head would fall, or even if they would move. Some fluid escaped from her little nose, which made me catch my breath.

'It's normal,' Danny soothed. He'd already warned me this might happen, but I don't think anything can prepare you for something like that and it still took me by surprise.

Standing there with Azaylia in my arms was incredibly tough, but it was also a moment to cherish forever. *Ah, my little baby*, I thought. I felt relief swim through my veins. My daughter was in my arms again and I was taking care of her.

Ever so slowly, I placed Azaylia into the casket. We'd given her a little pillow with orange buttons on it and I put her on her back, in the position she always liked to sleep in. She had to be comfortable and I made sure she was. The casket came with a little silk overlay blanket, but I took that out to keep so I could always feel the material Azaylia was surrounded by. Her favourite blanket was a pink and white marshmallow-coloured bobble blanket – we called it her 'comforty' blanket. I put that over her and snuggled her in.

There had been a moment, a few days before, when I was sitting with Azaylia and I sensed a shift in energy in the room. Her soul was leaving her body, I thought. I didn't dwell on it because Azaylia was still present, lying in front of me, and even if her soul had left the room, or the earth, it was still present, in the sky above.

Her soul had left her body now, for sure. I felt that profoundly. *She's not here anymore, it's time to say goodbye.* I could hear murmured conversations in the corridor outside and then Ashley appeared.

'Do you think I should come in?'

His mum and my brother Danny were there and he posed the question to the three of us. Inside I was thinking, *Please, please, please come in.* I desperately wanted Ashley to see Azaylia one last time, but it had to be his decision.

'What do *you* want to do?' I said.

He asked if she had changed much.

'Yes, she's changed,' I said.

I had to tell the truth. As the weeks went by, her face was not as plump and pink as it was, of course. But she was still Azaylia and she looked as cute as ever, still in her pink bobble hat and wearing her cosy lion suit and orange socks.

'I'll come in,' Ashley said, taking a deep breath.

My heart sang as he walked towards us. It was like a ray of sunshine came up from inside me and brightened the whole room. Azaylia would be with Mummy and Daddy again and that is what I wanted for her.

As Ashley leaned over the casket, I was holding my breath on his behalf, anxious as to how he would react.

'Wow,' he said, giving Azaylia a kiss, 'you're still as beautiful as ever.'

It was such a wonderful moment and I was so relieved and thankful. It felt exactly the right thing to do and I was so happy for Ashley.

We both placed our letters beside Azaylia and I showed Ashley the toys I was putting in with her. The replacement Simba and Nala soft toys I'd bought took pride of place and I put her original Simba and Nala in a bag, for us to keep. The toy mobile phone was there and the paper butterflies were dotted all around. I wanted him to see exactly what I'd done for Azaylia and I was pleased when he approved of everything. We were still Azaylia's parents – we always would be – and I wanted us to keep sharing all the decision-making, just like we always had.

Our three gold necklaces were waiting in separate jewellery boxes and we decided to put them on at the same time, as a family. We got Azaylia to kiss our necklaces, as if she'd blessed them, and we kissed hers before putting it around her neck. The last touch was to place the gold heart pendant printed with our three sets of fingerprints over Azaylia's heart.

She was finally ready now.

I closed my eyes as the lid went down.

I'm still here, Azaylia. You can't see me and I can't see you, but Mummy will always be here.

CHAPTER
TWENTY

The blinds were closed in the front room. I could hear the street starting to fill up with people and then I heard the sound of horses' hooves. Azaylia was here, arriving in her carriage. It was time to step outside, but I didn't want to go. My arms had weights on them and there were invisible forces all around my body, pulling me back.

I can't do it. I don't want to do it.

Two friends had kindly helped get me ready, doing my hair and make-up and even helping me get dressed and put on my shoes. I was so grateful to them. I felt weak and aggravated and detached from my body; I hadn't had to present myself properly to the world for so long and I'd forgotten how to do it. I was *incapable* of doing it by myself.

The night before I'd said my prayers like I always do and I took one of Azaylia's babygros to bed with me and gave it a kiss, the way I used to kiss Azaylia goodnight. I could still smell her scent and I slept deeply with it by my side. My brain was so exhausted, I just wanted to be away from myself and the world.

I'd been struggling from the second I opened my eyes. I hadn't stopped crying, but I *had* to get myself together now. I would be in Azaylia's presence when I stepped onto the street: this was Azaylia's Day and everything had to be perfect for her.

We'd planned the day meticulously; we wanted magic and serenity and purity and paradise – it was the last thing we could do for our daughter on earth. She wasn't going to be here for her first birthday party, but we could create a little bit of heaven on earth, surrounding her with as much beauty and light and warmth and happiness as we could possibly conjure. Azaylia was going to have Mummy and Daddy walking behind her cortège as it travelled down our road and through the town, and Mummy had to be strong and brave for her baby.

'Come on, we've got this,' Ashley said, locking his eyes on mine as he appeared at my side in the living room. He looked immaculate, dressed in a black suit with a bright orange tie and pocket handkerchief. His beard was long because Azaylia loved to play with it and so he didn't ever want to cut it, and he'd had a broken heart shaved into the back of his head. The finishing touch to my hair was to have gold clips spelling out 'Azaylia' across the back. We hadn't discussed either of these designs, but they complemented each other perfectly. When we sat in front of our friends and family during Azaylia's service, our messages would be on display, side by side – we couldn't have planned it better.

'Let's go,' I said, wiping the tears from my cheeks. Another good friend had done me bespoke nails in orange and pale pink, decorated with pictures of Azaylia, angel wings and Simba. They were more than a special tribute to Azaylia – I wanted to be able to see her face all day long, right there in front of me. I hadn't imagined I'd be using my nails the way I was now, to catch my tears and flick them away, so as not to ruin my make-up. But I'd promised Azaylia I would do her proud and look my very best, so I was trying my hardest to keep my word.

As the front door opened, I felt my whole body go numb. It was a gloomy, wet day, but Azaylia's small casket was shining bright inside her gleaming white carriage. I stared at her initials, written proudly on the orange panel on the side of the white casket. Everything looked so perfect, yet this was the saddest sight I'd ever seen.

Azaylia's cortège was being led by nine strong and graceful white horses, each with an orange plume in its mane and an orange sash across its back, also emblazoned with her initials. She was such a strong and powerful little girl and the magnificent horses represented the strength that was pulling her forward.

The street was so full of people you couldn't see a single space on the ground. I tried to look up but I couldn't see faces and my hearing had dimmed so much I could scarcely hear a sound. It felt like everybody had dissolved away in my tears, their voices shrinking away with them, and all I could see was Azaylia's glimmering casket, wrapped in its quiet oasis.

I took my place alongside Ashley, standing behind the carriage. The weights on my arms had become even heavier and I felt my whole body turn to stone. Ashley and me linked arms and started to move forward as one. Like a pair of stone statues, we walked on heavily, in step with one another just as we had done all the way along the road that brought us here. I stole a glance at him as we left our house behind. Tears were rolling down his frozen face. He looked scared and he was speechless with emotion: this was the last time Azaylia would be on this street and it didn't seem real.

I could feel the whole neighbourhood walking behind us, but my senses were so blurred I couldn't take in what I was experiencing. The horses were going fast and we had to walk at quite a pace, which took me aback. I was wearing a black military-style dress with a short cape and high black heels. It was the first time I'd worn heels in so long and my feet were hurting as I struggled to keep up.

I want this to stop! I wish this would stop.

I just wanted to drop to my knees and for everything to grind to a halt.

Further down the road, we got into black cars to continue Azaylia's journey through the town. I felt relieved to be off my feet, less exposed than when I was walking. The public had given us so much support and I was 100 per cent behind sharing Azaylia's day like this, but it was tough, nonetheless.

When we drove off, I finally started to see and hear what was going on around me. There were mums and dads, kids and teenagers and grandmas and grandads, all out to show their support, for mile after mile after mile. I could hear slow, respectful clapping and I could see hundreds of sad faces, stricken with grief. It was raining hard and it felt like the streets themselves were crying. 'Let's go, champ!' a lone voice shouted. People were out on their drives playing 'I Wanna Be Like You' on their soundboxes. Children were letting off orange balloons, there were pensioners and teenagers in orange tops and scarves and hats, and parents were holding their babies tight to their chests under orange umbrellas.

It struck me that, for so long, the people who supported us had been invisible, hidden behind the screens of mobile phones and laptops and iPads. We knew how much support we had in our community, but to see all these members of the public come from behind the screens was incredible. Orange ribbons were tied to trees and lamp posts, there were balloons in the shapes of rainbows and the letter 'A' and people were letting off orange flares high into the sky. It felt like the whole community had come out to hug us and they hugged us every inch of the way as the cortège made its steady journey through the town.

We had a cut-off point along the route, where we said goodbye to the public. The horses could only walk so far and we stopped in a private location so Azaylia could be carried into her special car to continue her journey. The rain was coming down hard, but in the brief moment when our daughter was carried out of her white carriage and into the car the rain held off.

Typical Azaylia, I thought, *doing more magic in the sky!*

There was a soft blanket waiting for her in the car, printed with photographs of Azaylia, Ashley and me. That would keep her company along the way, I thought. Her casket was flanked by teddy bears and two displays of pretty white flowers spelling out her name, one in each window. *Jungle Book* monkeys and *Lion King* teddies poked through each letter of her name. It was simple and childlike. I didn't want the car swamped with flowers – she was a little angel and I wanted her to have space to spread her wings.

The service was being held in the grounds of Ashley's auntie Michelle's house in Leicestershire. She has acres of land and very kindly offered to let us put up a large white marquee. It meant we could invite a few more people than if we held the service in an indoor venue and it fitted perfectly with our vision for the day.

Azaylia's Day was not about death, it was about heaven. We didn't want anything formal and we didn't want a traditional religious service in a dark, echoing building – Azaylia was a child and her day needed to be vibrant and bursting with light and life.

I thought I would fall to pieces when I watched the men carry Azaylia inside. Ashley and Danny were at the front and Ashley's two brothers, Matt and Ryan, were at the back. I followed behind with the women of the family. The girls were at my side, ready to catch me if I fell.

A fabulous rainbow balloon arch marked the entrance to the marquee and the *Aladdin* music 'A Whole New World' was playing as we stepped inside. The music was so poignant and fitting. That gave me some small comfort, though tears were streaming down my face. I glanced anxiously around the room, hoping our plans had come together. The marquee was decked with hundreds and hundreds of balloons. Life-size models of a lion, a giraffe and an elephant took pride of pride in amongst the jungle theme at the front and angel wings hung above a spectacular chandelier in the centre. Beautiful, bright and light, it felt like a haven from the dismal weather outside. I sighed with relief.

When we first started to plan Azaylia's Day, we hadn't anticipated darkness and rain in late May 2021, but the forecast was awful all day long. It didn't matter now – the weather only made Azaylia's white paradise appear brighter still. We'd created a perfect venue, I thought. *This is all for you, princess.* It was exactly the piece of heaven on earth we wanted to give her.

Family and friends were already seated, but as I walked to the front, I couldn't take in who was where. Their clothes formed a sea of black and there were orange reflections glinting on the waves. Ashley and me took our places on a small orange velvet settee, facing Azaylia. She was right there in front of us, which is exactly what we wanted. We didn't want to leave her lying alone in her casket, out of our reach. Throughout the service, we would be within touching distance, watching over her as we always had.

A celebrant led tributes to Azaylia, showing all our favourite pictures on a giant screen. It was a beautiful way to start the ceremony and he did a wonderful job of encapsulating Azaylia's strength and courage and the incredible fight she put up. We smiled and we cried, but all the while I was in so much pain my heart was physically aching in my chest. Ashley and me gave each other squeezes and little touches of love: *I'm here*, they said. *I'm with you, I care, I love you.* The longer the service went on, the more I started to feel afraid. We were getting closer to the moment when we would have to lay Azaylia to rest and I felt cold little shivers running across my chest.

Ashley stood up to give his address and my heart went out to him. His eyes were swollen from crying and he looked shattered and weary.

'My daughter, Azaylia Diamond Cain, was special,' he started. 'Beautiful. Strong. Courageous and so, so inspirational. I don't think that a single person in this room can say they're too wise, educated or experienced to have not learned something meaningful from my little lion. From the second that she came into my life everything changed. She changed my life. She saved my life and she made my life.'

His voice was breaking and he began to falter. I wanted to rush up and give him a hug or offer to help, but I knew Ashley would want to stand strong for Azaylia, on his own two feet. The fact Azaylia's diagnosis collided with Covid meant we were both very used to pushing through alone, even in the darkest of moments. Ashley was representing his daughter here. He was talking as a man and as a daddy and he would get through this on his own.

And so he gritted his teeth and carried on, describing in touching detail how he missed waking up in the morning in hospital and seeing Azaylia lying in her cot, not crying or screaming, but waiting patiently for Daddy to wake up so she could give him a massive, beautiful smile. He also described how I used to tell him to leave Azaylia alone sometimes because he couldn't stop showering her with kisses. My heart was pounding with love for him, he was doing so well.

I could hear people crying and sniffing all around me. The room had gone to pieces and Ashley was on the edge again. *We're all family here*, I was thinking. *If you crumble and fall to the floor, we're all here to pick you up.*

Ashley went on to talk about the Disney film *Coco* and how it had resonated deeply with him, teaching him about Mexican traditions and how our journey to the 'other side' should not be viewed as some 'unavoidable terror', but something to treasure: 'As long as our loved ones are remembered here on earth,' he said, 'they will live on for eternity in paradise.'

He had promised Azaylia he would make her name live on. 'I will carry her name to the stars,' he said. 'I will be a vessel and help other families and poorly children until it's my final journey and then, hopefully then, I will be at peace and I will be happy as I will have earned my place in heaven where I'll be with you, my baby, once again.'

His every word was spoken with profound passion and the love and grief in the room was palpable.

'To the top of every mountain, to the bottom of every valley, along every road, across every ocean,' he continued. 'North to south, east to west, corner to corner, pillar to post, I'll take you there, baby. Let's go, champ. My champion. My world. My hero. Azaylia Diamond Cain, I love you.'

Wow.

It took me a moment before I could breathe again. Ashley had done Azaylia proud: it was the speech of his life. I watched as he knelt beside Azaylia in her casket and cried. There was music and a father's poem to listen to while we all gathered ourselves together. Ashley had chosen Michael Bolton's 'Go the Distance' from the Disney film *Hercules*. The lyrics, about being strong and finding your way, were perfect.

Now it was my turn to get up and speak.

Mummy will stand strong for you, I said silently to Azaylia as I rose to my feet. *I've got this, baby.*

I was incredibly nervous and my hands were trembling. I'd only prepared what I wanted to say the night before because I knew I was incapable of doing it until the very last minute. It was my final act of resistance to reality, I suppose, and I only put pen to paper when my self-denial ran out of road and I had no choice but to accept this day had come.

I was breathing heavily as I took my place at the front, looking out at our loved ones and sweeping my eyes across Azaylia's casket. 'I got this, come on, Azaylia,' I said out loud, trying to hold myself together. 'Stay with Mummy.'

I was ready now, or at least as ready as I'd ever be.

'With my beautiful daughter, Azaylia Diamond Cain,' I started, my voice shaking out of control. 'The day I found out I was pregnant …' The tears started springing to my eyes and my words were suddenly trapped in my throat. 'I'm sorry,' I stuttered. 'I'm so sorry …'

Ashley was by my side in an instant. 'Take your time,' he whispered. 'Breathe.' He said I could do it and then he asked me quietly if I wanted him to stay up there and help. I gave him a brave smile, wiped my tears and asked him to take a seat before clearing my throat and trying again, determined to continue this time.

My speech was very different to Ashley's. I summarised the highs and lows of our journey, talking about my joy at giving birth and finding what was missing from my life, and then all too quickly seeing my world shatter when Azaylia received her diagnosis. I told everyone that the days I spent with my daughter were the best of my life and I remembered her smiles and her strength of character and celebrated how she hit all her milestones and beat the odds, again and again.

'You're amazing,' I told Azaylia. 'You made me the woman I am now and I'm so thankful to you. I've never had a hero, Azaylia, or someone I look up to, but I've now found my hero, my beautiful, strong daughter. The only one who knows what my heart sounds like from the inside.'

I ended by talking about Whitney Houston's 'When You Believe', and how I sang it to Azaylia on the last night we went to sleep together. I also said she was in heaven now, dancing and singing and watching us. 'I love you, Azaylia, forever and always. I will have you in my heart forever, but now, half of my heart lives in heaven. Until we're together again, when we'll be in heaven together. My darling daughter, Azaylia Diamond Cain, Mummy loves you.'

I wanted to sing 'When You Believe' to her one last time and, when the music started, I got to my knees in front of Azaylia and hugged her in her casket, singing every single word to her. I never wanted to let go.

We had a mother's poem next, followed by a montage of videos and written tributes from family and friends. They spoke about how inspirational Azaylia was and how much they loved her. It was wonderful to see so much love beaming from the screen in front of us. Azaylia could not have wished for a more loving support network all around her. The service had been everything we had wished for, and more – we had all done her proud.

'Dancing in the Sky' by Beverly Ann was playing as we left the marquee, and I rang a bell, which was a reminder of how Azaylia had fought so hard to ring the bell and leave hospital. The atmosphere was calm and serene, but inside my head a noisy storm was raging. *Ahhhh! No! I don't want to do it! I want to stay here!* It was time to take Azaylia to her final resting place and I was absolutely petrified. I'd seen my daughter every day while she was on earth and now she was going into the ground, in her casket. It was unfathomable and terrifying; cold shivers across my chest turned to icy footsteps, marching heavily on my heart.

How could I watch this happen, and how was I going to live without seeing my baby's face again? But the forces pulling me back into the house this morning were now pushing me forward: *Come on, it's time*, they said. And they wouldn't take no for an answer.

CHAPTER
TWENTY-ONE

What if Azaylia's going in a dark corner, stuck out of the way as if she's been forgotten? The idea terrified me as we made our way to the cemetery. We'd bought a plot for three so that Ashley and me could rest with Azaylia when our time came. It was next to the children's section, we'd been told, but as we drew closer I realised I didn't know exactly where that was. My anxiety was spiking and I was so annoyed with myself for missing this detail and not checking this out in advance.

I could see 'Azaylia's Garden' – that's what we were calling it – as soon as we pulled into the gates. *Thank God*, I thought, my fears subsiding a fraction. Right at the front in a wide, open part of the cemetery, it was surrounded by beautiful mature trees that didn't cast a shadow. It was perfect for her and I was so relieved. This garden was her forever home, a sacred place of sanctuary and paradise – I felt so much more at peace for seeing it.

We'd had a small marquee put over the plot to keep Azaylia dry as she was laid to rest. It was raining heavily when we stepped out of the cars, but guess what? When Azaylia was carried out, there was another break in the weather and it was barely spitting – it was as if someone had pressed stop, just long enough for Azaylia to make her entrance in style.

Taking my place in the garden, I felt frozen to the bone. People were coming up to me and offering condolences, but I didn't want anyone to come near me. I just wanted to be left alone with my thoughts and grief. After spending so long isolated in hospital, I wasn't used to being around so many people and I didn't feel comfortable. I felt as cold as ice; the only person I wanted to be near, and to hold, was my baby.

My heart was breaking into a million pieces as Azaylia was lowered into her forever home. I could picture her clearly inside her casket and I was reminding myself that I had dressed her in comfortable clothes and wrapped her in favourite blanket. Her body was rested and peaceful, she had her keepsakes and her toys all around her. There was a photograph of me and Ashley and Azaylia alongside her letters and she had her pretty butterflies and her phone.

I said my prayers over and over again and I repeated, 'I love you, baby, you're OK. You're in paradise now and it's beautiful.'

Azaylia's resting place was lined with bricks and tiles so her casket was well protected. I reminded myself of that too. She *was* well protected, because her soul was in heaven now. I looked up at the sky. *She's up there*, I thought. *Her spirit is there, in the sky*. Azaylia was in paradise, so there was no need to worry about a thing.

We had brought a single rose each for family and friends to put on top of Azaylia's casket, if they wanted to, and me and Ashley had a basket with three doves in, which we released to the universe. 'Be free!' we said. Our spirits would always fly together, no matter where we were.

I started to hear people talking around me and they were saying things like 'I wish it was me,' or 'I wish I could swap places.' Everyone meant well, of course they did, but I was hypersensitive and comments like that were making me feel anxious and paranoid. People would only say that if they didn't think Azaylia was in paradise, wouldn't they? So where did they think she was? Where was she?

I disregarded any remarks that put me on edge and I kept my protective barriers firmly up. Azaylia was definitely in paradise now, where she deserved to be. Nobody was going to shake me off balance and dislodge that belief from my head.

We had a steel band playing as this part of the day drew to a close. It was the sound of tropical paradise and it made me melt into myself. I'd been like a pressure cooker all day long, but now my feelings were starting to bubble and break loose. It was a weird sensation. I could feel my emotions dislodging themselves from places deep inside me; they were percolating to the surface and I had no control switch. My heart felt like it was being slashed with a knife, time and time again, releasing other feelings I also had no control over.

I knew it was time to leave the cemetery. The cars were waiting to take us back to the marquee, but I stood rooted next to Azaylia, clutching her Nala teddy. I didn't want to leave and as the pressure and tension escaped from my body I started to break down. I could finally be myself now and true to my real feelings. Azaylia was in her resting place and I didn't have to put on my bravest smile any longer. My pain was pouring out of me. Distraught, I began sobbing loudly and uncontrollably, howling into the rain.

Ashley and Danny and the girls in the family were by my side, and other members of the close family were behind. I could feel them circling, coming to take care of me. It was like watching myself in one of those dreams where you're about to fall off a cliff or get run over by a car. You know you'll wake up in a minute and go 'phew!', but I didn't. I was still here. I could feel a hand on my shoulder and someone clasping my hand, but the more the pressure escaped from my body, the louder I sobbed and cried. The family's warmth was radiating off them, but I still had invisible walls around me and I didn't want anyone to come through them.

Ashley turned in to me. He knew what I needed and he gave me my space and started walking to the cars. As I glanced over my shoulder, I could see the family waiting with him. I was the last person standing with Azaylia now and I must have looked so vulnerable and alone standing there. My loved ones wanted to take me into their cocoon and carry me away, but I wasn't ready yet. There was a giant magnet keeping me by Azaylia's side – it was that mummy magnet again, pulling me in to my daughter.

I didn't want to take my eyes off Azaylia's casket. I brought her into this world and I wanted to be the last one to say my prayers with her. I wasn't saying goodbye, this was not goodbye. I was very clear about that in my mind and I wasn't using that word. *I wish I could jump in the ground with you*, I thought, but I knew I had work to do before I could join Azaylia. I had to become more like her and earn my place in heaven. Only then could I be with her again.

When I eventually tore my feet off the ground and walked away, I felt so bereft and disorientated. My identity had changed, irreversibly. I felt that very strongly. I would always be Azaylia's mummy, but I was an angel mummy now. I no longer had a duty of care to my daughter on earth and that devastated me.

* * *

The marquee at Auntie Michelle's had been re-set, with all the chairs moved around, tables installed and pink and white streamers hanging from the roof. It looked amazing, but I didn't want to be back here. It had felt like the longest day already and I was in no mood to celebrate Azaylia's life in the way we had planned, with as much joy and laughter as possible.

People needed to eat. We had Caribbean food – I love Caribbean food – and it looked and smelled so good. I felt weak and light-headed and I knew I needed to have some food, but after I filled my plate I couldn't bring myself to eat more than a mouthful. I wanted to curl up in a corner and close my eyes, but I had to go on.

I looked around the room. Other people were eating and smiling, showing each other videos and pictures they had on their phones of Azaylia. Some were crying, holding their head in their hands, and other family members were comforting them.

I watched my little nephew with pride. He'd been with us all day and was doing so well. Even though he was only four, my brother felt it was important Noah shared the whole day. Danny wanted him to see that Azaylia was sleeping in her garden now and he wanted to teach his son that passing to the other side is part of life and it's what happens to us all.

I can still remember the moment the dance music came on. Azaylia loved music, of course she did. She was comforted by it and it brought her so much pleasure when she danced in her daddy's arms. I'd appreciated hearing 'A Whole New World' when Azaylia arrived at the marquee this morning. It felt right to surround our daughter with such a poignant and beautiful song. But she wasn't in the room with us now, was she? Everything had changed and I suddenly had a very strong reaction to what I was hearing: 'Turn the music off!' I wanted to scream. 'Get that music off!' People were taking to the dance floor and they were smiling and celebrating Azaylia's life, just as we hoped they would. But something had changed inside me, now that my baby was in her garden.

Stop! She's not here! We don't need to do this anymore!

I had so much pain and heartache rising inside me. I was trying to reason with myself, and I reminded myself what Ashley had said when we were making all our plans for the day.

'Azaylia needs to see us dance, Safiyya. She needs to dance with us.'

Music was Ashley's thing. It had played a huge part in his life with Azaylia – it had in mine too – and there was no question that music wouldn't feature heavily on Azaylia's Day. But I felt very differently now we were actually here, and our daughter wasn't, and I was struggling like mad to deal with it.

Ashley was on the dance floor with his close family, all commemorating Azaylia's life the best way they knew how. Ashley's got some great moves and everyone was encouraging him to breakdance, knowing how much he normally enjoys it. I could see his eyes were still heavy with sadness, but he was joining in and he was smiling and laughing as he fed off the huge amount of love surrounding him.

I couldn't start changing everything now, could I? It was out of the question. But the more the music played on, the more I felt I didn't want to do this anymore. I wanted to pull the plug, not just on the music, but also on the rest of the day.

'Stop!' I wanted to shout. 'I want this to stop!'

I reminded myself how proud I was of the fact Azaylia had only ever been around positive energy. She didn't see misery and depression and she didn't hear raised voices. I only ever cried when she couldn't see me and as soon as she was in the room it was 'click!' and my smile was back, just like turning on a light switch.

You've come this far, a voice in my head was saying. *You can't lose your shit now.*

Why not? I countered. I was already losing it and had been since the cemetery.

Club 100 had closed down, I thought. Concealing my emotions was not going to help Azaylia anymore and I was so done with it.

Ashley had no idea how I was feeling – how could he? He came over to pull me up to dance and for a second I felt like digging my heels into the floor and refusing.

What would Azaylia do? What would Azaylia think? These were the questions that ultimately helped me stay the course. Even though I was struggling, it was unthinkable that my daughter would look down and think, *Mummy's not doing my day the way she promised she would.*

I had a little dance with Ashley, and I'm so glad I did. I was swamped with sadness but I started to take comfort from the fact we were sticking to the plan and doing what we wanted to do, for Azaylia.

Towards the end of the night we asked everybody to get their coat and stand in the garden, in front of the rainbow balloon arch. *The Lion King* 'Circle of Life' started playing and then a dazzling display of orange and pink fireworks began to light up the sky. We'd managed to keep this a surprise, and everyone was totally bowled over.

'Let's go, champ!' someone shouted, which started a whole chorus of shouts and cheers: 'We love you, Azaylia!', 'Keep shining bright!'

I enjoyed the fireworks. We wanted to light up the sky for Azaylia and we succeeded. It was also a chance for everyone to let it all out and scream into the night. There wasn't a dry eye and at last I allowed myself to step into the circle and be wrapped in love from all the family.

Afterwards, I sat on a sofa at the back of the marquee with my brother and two close friends. Danny talked about the good times we had had with Azaylia and managed to make me laugh and I shared stories that brought smiles to all of our faces, remembering how Azaylia wanted to put her face in the trifle on Christmas Day and how she used to beat up her Emily doll. There were lots of tears between the laughter and then, eventually, I just started to sob. And I kept on sobbing until my head eventually landed on my pillow and my heavy eyes could finally rest.

I'd given everything I had and now I was totally done.

CHAPTER TWENTY-TWO

The bedroom was eerily quiet when I opened my eyes.

You're not here, are you, Azaylia?

I blinked around anxiously as the grains of sleep left my eyes, already knowing her place beside me was empty. *I will never snuggle her soft body or smell her sweet head again. I can't see her beautiful smile light up the room.*

Waking up and remembering had become a recurring torture, but today the feelings of loss and pain cut deeper than ever before. I couldn't go to the Chapel of Rest to give Azaylia a kiss and tell her I loved her. There was no casket to design, no balloons to pick out or decisions to be made about doves or white horses.

Azaylia was in her garden, and everything was done now.

I'd slept deeply but my head was still heavy as stone. It felt like someone was standing on my heart and that I'd never be able to lift myself out of bed again. I didn't need to, anyhow, because who was I, without Azaylia to care for? What was the point of my life?

Ashley had got up but the whole house was too quiet. His familiar sounds had faded away. There was no music or singing. All I could hear from downstairs were soft footsteps and a door slowly opening and closing.

We were in a different kind of survival mode now. When I finally pulled myself out of bed – I don't know how – I could barely get showered and dressed. Ashley was in a similar state. We didn't know what to do or how to cope, and we just stayed in the house together, existing as best we could.

For most of the day I sat on the settee in the lounge, crying and feeling numb all over. I kissed Azaylia's photographs and ate the food the family kindly made us, but only out of necessity. I had no appetite for anything. The light had gone out of our lives, we were in a void of darkness and despair.

We visited her garden and I felt peace wash over me as soon as we arrived. It gave me so much solace to be close to Azaylia again and after that I began to visit every day, several times a day, sitting alone or with Ashley and other family members who came and went. I'd get a coffee and sit and talk to her, sometimes for hours.

At night we spent ages looking up to the sky, waiting for the stars to come out. There was one on the right-hand side of our house that always powered through. We hadn't spotted it before Azaylia passed and now we were waiting for it every night.

'There she is!' we'd say. 'Shining bright! Dazzling like the diamond that you are! We love you, baby!'

On cloudy nights we'd still look out and talk to her. 'Are you hiding, Azaylia? Are you playing peek-a-boo? We know you're there!'

Then I couldn't wait for the day to be over, so I could shut my eyes and escape into nothingness, for as long as I possibly could.

. . .

Whenever I spoke to close family members I tried to appear stronger than I was. I'd tell them I'd seen Azaylia in the sky, or I talked about the support I was getting online and from the local community. That was how I was used to dealing with things and I didn't want to burden my loved ones with my grief because they were all grieving too.

My followers had been absolutely incredible, posting poems about grief and motivational messages for me to read, and the most thoughtful gifts were still arriving. Children's drawings came through the door, along with candles with poignant inscriptions and some amazing sketches and paintings of Azaylia with Mummy and Daddy. There were personalised plaques and ornaments for her garden too and I knew that was where I needed to spend even more of my time. Azaylia's Garden was a haven and it was the one place on earth where I could be a hands-on mummy and do some mummy duties again.

The flowers from the car that spelled out Azaylia were propped up beside her, and friends and relatives had brought some incredible floral tributes, including a large orange lion and an angel. We'd had so many flowers delivered to the house that I had to buy buckets to put them in and people were laying more and more flowers in the garden every day. But there was no structure or design to the garden yet, and I realised that was where I needed to focus my energy.

'Her garden should be lit,' I said. 'Azaylia gave us light, and light is what she deserves to be surrounded by.'

As soon as I said this, I knew I had a purpose again and that felt good. I would make it my mission to create the most beautiful garden possible for Azaylia and I would work so hard and make her proud of her mummy.

We had to wait for the soil to settle before we could do any proper landscaping, but I went to B&M and Asda, scoured their garden aisles and bought packs and packs of solar lights. Then I went on Amazon and bought pretty rainbow and angel solar lights too.

'You won't be in the dark at night any more,' I told Azaylia. 'The angels will shine their lights and they will watch over you.'

I've never been green-fingered, but I was determined I was going to turn Azaylia's Garden into the prettiest patch of paradise imaginable. 'No, don't put that there,' I started to say when people laid flowers and ornaments down in no particular order. The family cottoned on quickly. 'We'll just leave these here for you, Safiyya,' they said, taking a step back. 'You put them where you think best.' They were giving me space to do my thing, but keeping an eye on me too. I appreciated their tact and care. The garden had become my reason to live and I needed to be in charge of it.

Ashley had started cycling a lot, pushing himself to go faster and further. Fitness had always been his therapy, but he preferred to be out in the elements now instead of inside a gym. When he was outdoors he felt connected to the sky and therefore to Azaylia – 'She can see me,' he said. 'She can hear me and she can be with me while I train.'

He'd started taking ice baths too. His focus was zoning in on Azaylia's foundation now – that was giving him purpose and a reason to get up in the morning. He was having conversations about how to move forward and how he wanted to raise even more money by taking on some incredibly tough personal challenges. Whatever he put himself through, it would be nothing compared to what Azaylia had endured. Children with cancer were his heroes now and his mission in life was to help them and their families in any way he could.

.   .   .

In the days and weeks following Azaylia's Day, I started seeing orange sunsets again. They'd taken a little break, but now they were back with a vengeance, lighting up the sky behind her garden. Rainbows were appearing again too, arching above her and pulsing with colour and light.

'Look at Azaylia,' I said to family and friends who came and sat with me. 'She's looking down on us. Hello, Azaylia! How are you doing today, princess?'

No one in my close circle ever challenged my beliefs about heaven. Why would they? They shared and supported my views and they could see how much comfort I was taking from the skies, just as Ashley was. They didn't question how much time I was spending in the garden either, because it was obvious it was keeping me alive and it brought solace to them too.

I got to know some of the other people who visited their loved ones at the cemetery. All the locals had heard about Azaylia and that made it easier for me to talk to them, because I didn't have to explain our story.

'Do you come here every day?' a man asked me one afternoon. I'd seen him and his wife visiting their granddaughter's resting place often.

'Yes, sometimes twice a day, or three times,' I told him.

'I used to do that,' he said, 'but then someone told me it wasn't good for me and I should come less often.'

I was irritated and confused, and asked, 'Did you *like* coming every day?'

'Well, yes,' he said. 'I did.'

I told him, if it was what he wanted to do, he should do it. What was wrong with sitting with your granddaughter and having a cup of coffee if that's what you wanted to do? Did people who went to a coffee shop every day have other people interfering and telling them it was wrong?

The tension I felt on Azaylia's Day was still bubbling under my skin. If anyone had an opinion on the afterlife that I didn't want to hear, I was short with them or I walked away. I hadn't been offered any counselling since leaving the hospital, but looking back, maybe this was the time I needed it?

I didn't know anything about the grieving process, but what I did recognise was that, despite the comfort the garden and the skies were giving me, I wasn't getting any better. When I was on my own I would sit for hours on end, crying and crying and feeling myself slowly crumbling inside. I didn't want to take anti-depressants – they always made me think of the tenants who used to come round my childhood home, asking Mum for their tablets, and how it baffled me that they were taking medicine but never getting better – I wasn't going to go down that route, I wanted to work through this on my own.

I started to process the fact that, while she was ill, I'd taken all my strength from Azaylia. *She* gave me all the strength I needed to get this far, but now that my responsibilities to her on earth were over, my strength was deteriorating. I didn't discuss this with anyone. I didn't want to burden my loved ones when they were all broken too, so I just tried to carry on the way I knew best, chasing orange skies and rainbows and talking to the brightest star in the sky.

●　●　●

'Happy Father's Day!' I cheered.

Ashley had just come in from a morning run and I'd prepared a surprise for him, turning the living room orange with a light projector. When he walked in the door 'I Wanna Be Like You' was playing with the volume turned up high. He stopped in his tracks. 'I don't know what to say,' he blurted. 'Oh my God, Safiyya! This is so special.' He started crying and I gave him a hug. 'Thank you, Safiyya,' he said. 'Thank you so much.'

We'd decided we wanted to mark the day by spending it with Azaylia, doing her garden. A month had passed since Azaylia's Day and the soil had finally bedded down, which meant we could turn the earth over and landscape it properly, something we'd been waiting to do.

As another surprise I'd ordered in a luxury picnic to take to Azaylia's, full of sandwiches and sausage rolls and gorgeous little cakes, and I had a beautiful teddy bear made out of orange flowers to place as a centrepiece in her garden. Ashley was bowled over and it was so good to see him smile. He'd found it very hard to sleep the night before and clearly this was going to be such a tough day for him. I wanted to give him hugs of warmth throughout the day, to make the underlying sadness more bearable.

'Here's your present, from Azaylia,' I said.

He laughed – it was boxers emblazoned with 'Best Daddy in the World'. I'd written him a card too, filling it with beautiful words and telling him what an incredible daddy he was. I meant every word – Ashley was becoming more incredible by the day, working tirelessly towards setting up Azaylia's charity. At first I'd been lagging behind him, but now I was expressing my views and starting to take part in meetings about the way forward. We had more than £1.5 million in the GoFundMe account, which was a huge sum to deal with. We'd never done anything like this before and we had a lot of work to do, from registering with the Charity Commission to creating budgets and policies, building a brand and working with medical institutions and doctors to develop the most effective foundation possible.

Ashley and me would give our time for free, of course. This was our passion and purpose, not a paid job of work. That meant we'd also need to recruit a CEO to run the charity professionally, which was another huge job in itself.

One thing we were both clear on, right from the start, was that we wanted Azaylia's foundation to have longevity. Our aim was not only to help individual children reach their life-saving goals, but to invest in cancer research and innovative treatments to revolutionise cancer care and treatment options for children fighting cancer here in the UK.

I was pushing myself every day, doing whatever I could to help support Ashley and get the charity up and running. It gave me an important purpose in life and it became the best motivator imaginable. I was doing the work Azaylia prepared me to do and the charity was a powerful way of staying connected to her. That's what I'd wanted and it was exciting to see our dreams slowly start to turn into reality.

. . .

When we arrived at the garden that day there were bundles of orange balloons around Azaylia as yet another surprise for Ashley and a big clear balloon filled with confetti and 'Happy 1st Father's Day Daddy' painted on the side in orange. This was the first of many Father's Days – we'd celebrate them every single year. As Ashley said, Azaylia may have only held his hand for a short while, but she would hold her daddy's heart forever.

We put music on and toiled for hours, putting down artificial grass and edging and arranging all the pretty decorations and solar lights around Azaylia. It looked amazing and we were both buzzing afterwards. Being busy and working hard were a healthy distraction for us both and I wanted to keep on filling the day with little treats and distractions so that Ashley's heart wouldn't have time to sink, or at least not for too long.

'Surprise!' I said again when we got home. It was time for another present – a pair of pyjamas that said 'Superdad' across the chest. Ashley smiled when he put them on – my mission had been accomplished.

It hadn't been easy going shopping for Father's Day. I tried not to look at the little children who were picking out presents for their daddies, just as I avoided the baby aisle when I went in Asda. I'd strayed into it by accident one day and found myself crying uncontrollably, desperately looking for the exit through blurry eyes. Now I planned my route around the store, careful to swerve the baby section at all costs. It was the same in Tesco, where I was always reminded of the early days when I was buying baby milk and Infacol, blissfully unaware of what was about to unfold. I couldn't cope with seeing other mums and babies with trollies full of nappies and baby food either – it had become second nature to look the other way, quicken my pace and rush past.

Azaylia's bedroom was still untouched for similar reasons. All her toys and equipment were sitting there quietly and clothes she never had the chance to grow into were still hanging in the wardrobe. I always washed her clothes and bedding in Fairy and I couldn't bear to use the brand again. Even the slightest whiff transported me back in time, triggering an avalanche of grief and longing.

• • •

Ashley had wanted to be smart on Father's Day, as a mark of respect to Azaylia, and before we went to her garden he'd changed into tweed trousers and a waistcoat along with a flat cap, his orange tie and a pair of wellies. He looked great and I told him so, which I could see he appreciated. Little kindnesses went a long way. That was something I'd been noticing a lot lately. My confidence and self-esteem were still very fragile, but a compliment from Ashley or a kind word from a stranger could make or break my day and I was making a conscious effort to make other people feel better in any way I could, despite my pain and grief. That was one of the gifts Azaylia had given me: smiles and kindness cost nothing and *everybody* benefited.

Before I was a mum I was always rushing through my days, thinking about which pair of shoes I wanted to buy next, or which handbag or car I was going to save up for. I wasn't a bad person, but I was focused on myself, what I wanted to achieve and where I wanted to be. Having Azaylia had broadened my horizons in ways I never imagined. I was less narrow-minded now and determined to be a bigger and better person. Azaylia was guiding me every day and I loved being able to look up to the sky and tell her: 'I want to be like you, Azaylia. You're my hero and my inspiration. You taught me this, princess. Thank you.' I was taking small steps towards earning my place beside her and I was ready to take a million more.

CHAPTER
TWENTY-THREE

The rain is barrelling down on my face and the wind is blowing me backwards. It's 30 September 2021 and I'm about to start my ascent of Scafell Pike, England's highest mountain. I've never climbed a mountain before and I never imagined I would. I'm scared about how difficult it will be, physically and emotionally, but determined to get to the summit. Azaylia has brought me here and I've promised her that I'm going to meet her at the top. Ashley will be there too, and so Mummy and Daddy and Azaylia will all be together again, high in the sky.

I pull up the sleeve of my waterproof jacket – orange, of course – and look at my right arm for inspiration. A few weeks earlier, for my birthday, I'd had a big tattoo of Azaylia's face, covering the inside of my forearm. The picture the tattoo artist copied was taken after Azaylia had just woken up from one of the countless general anaesthetics she endured. Her first reaction when she opened her eyes took me by surprise, because Azaylia looked at me and gave me a big, beautiful smile. It melted my heart and I wanted to carry that image with me always. My tattoo was a permanent reminder to stay strong and brave, just like my hero Azaylia. I could look at it whenever I wanted and see the smile that lit up the world.

I'm drawing strength and courage from it now as I stand at the foot of the mountain, a small support team around me. I give Azaylia a big smile back and plant a kiss on her cheek: 'I've got this little champ here with me and I'm gonna take her all the way to the top of the mountain,' I declare. 'Let's go, champ!'

The vastness of the landscape is mesmerising me. The mountain is a strong and powerful force of nature, just like Azaylia, and I try to embrace the wind and the cold as I start my climb. I can feel my mind blowing open as I put one foot in front of the other, so many thoughts and fears are breaking free as I follow the rugged path. So much has happened in the last few months and I let my memories roam loose in the wide-open space all around me.

· · ·

'Happy Birthday, baby! One today! Mummy loves you!'

I can see all the family in Azaylia's Garden, letting off balloons and singing 'Happy Birthday'. Ashley is leading the singing, which I'm so pleased to see. Neither of us had been sure what to do to mark the occasion. We were dreading it for weeks, but as 10 August 2021 drew closer, I decided I wanted to have some sort of a celebration for Azaylia. Ashley really wasn't sure – he didn't know how it was going to sit with him – but I told him I had to do *something*, even if it was just the two of us at home, showing Azaylia that she still had a birthday and that we were not going to let it go by unnoticed.

Our community of followers wanted to acknowledge her birthday too because they started asking what I was doing and offering help and advice and wonderful ideas to make the day special. I was so grateful because their support helped us move in the right direction. A man who'd followed our story offered to make a lion cake and he drove for miles to deliver a spectacular two-foot-high Simba-shaped cake to our door. Then a lady I met on Instagram offered to make beautiful *Lion King* biscuits and cakes with edible pictures of Azaylia on top. Others suggested we could have packets of popcorn with Azaylia stickers on them and a beautiful little champagne cart so everyone could raise a toast. The party had started to organise itself and, in the end, I got someone in to help me pull it all together.

'If nobody wants to come, that's fine,' I said to Ashley. 'I understand it might be a bit surreal but it's Azaylia's first birthday and this is what I want to do.' He was with me now. Still, right up until the last minute I had no idea if it really would be just me and Ashley, sitting with a couple of close family members in the living room.

Of course it wasn't. All the family turned up at the house and we celebrated together before going to Azaylia's Garden. The cousins had brought a beautiful rainbow arch and quite a crowd was gathered. I was really enjoying having all this warmth and joy and love around Azaylia, it was exactly what she deserved.

The highlight came after we sang 'Happy Birthday' and let off the balloons when everyone joined in with 'I Wanna Be Like You', singing at the tops of their voices. I could hear Ashley's voice louder than anyone else's and my heart sang too – that's when I knew for sure we'd made exactly the right decision.

It was my 34th birthday five days later and, to be brutally honest, I felt really shit. The previous year I didn't open my cards and presents until the evening because Azaylia was there, but I was blissfully happy: her presence was the only gift I wanted. I can remember laying her on her front across my lap, rubbing her little back and thinking how incredibly lucky I was to be her mum: 'I'm finally a woman! I'm finally a proper grown-up! Look at me with my beautiful baby!' My new life had started; the life I always dreamed of but never quite believed would come true. But looking back, I wasn't a grown-up, I didn't have a clue – my real growing up was all about to start.

Ashley knew how low I was feeling before my birthday now and he took me out for food. I tried my best to enjoy it but I was suffering so much inside. It was impossible to believe what had happened in the past twelve months. *How was Azaylia not here anymore? How had she been through so much and fought so bravely, yet she still wasn't in my arms?* The future felt so uncertain. I had my tattoo of Azaylia's face, which I loved, but I still felt so empty and bereft. We'd both been working hard for Azaylia's foundation and it was almost ready to launch. We were going to do amazing things with it, but where was the happiness at home? I didn't want another baby. I *had* a daughter. I only wanted Azaylia and I didn't ever want her to think I'd tried to replace her. I felt quite sure about that, but how would Ashley and me be without the family life we'd dreamed of?

When we got home from the restaurant Ashley surprised me with a birthday party. Once again, our living room was filled with family and friends and there were pictures of Azaylia hanging on ribbons from balloons on the ceiling. This time we had little shots and party music and I had the most beautiful birthday cake. It was fun and I loved it all, but the best part was that Ashley arranged it for me. Normally I was the party organiser and I was so touched that he'd gone to so much trouble to make it special.

. . .

We officially launched The Azaylia Foundation at the end of August 2021, in time for World Cancer Month in September. 'Fearless in the fight against children's cancer' was our motto and, after months of hard work behind the scenes, our mission was now clearly defined: 'The Azaylia Foundation aims to support families that are fundraising for treatments that may not be readily available on the NHS.'

On 31 August, Ashley and me were invited onto ITV's *Lorraine* to talk about Azaylia's legacy. I was incredibly nervous – who doesn't have nerves when they go live on daytime TV for the first time? – but my passion for the foundation and what we wanted to achieve trumped everything. We were honouring our daughter's name and we had a huge platform at our feet. I had to be brave like Azaylia and seize this opportunity with both hands. Christine Lampard was hosting that day and she was so lovely. I'd never met her before, but she was very warm and kind, helping me settle down on the sofa. I held my nerve, thank God, telling her how I wanted to raise awareness about children's cancer. Ashley was brilliant, getting his message across with great poise and passion. It had been an incredibly emotional experience and, as soon as we came off air, I burst into tears.

'I'll be back in a minute, princess,' I said to Azaylia, wiping my tears. 'You go out and play.' It was a little coping mechanism I'd started to use, which allowed me to cry when I needed to without feeling guilty that I was letting Azaylia down, or making her worried or sad when she looked down on me.

•   •   •

Ashley was determined to be true to the promise he made on Azaylia's Day: 'to the top of every mountain, to the bottom of every valley, along every road, across every ocean. North to south, east to west, corner to corner, pillar to post. I'll take you there, baby.' The first fundraising challenge he set himself was to cycle over 1,000 miles from Land's End to John o' Groats, all in just two weeks. *That's nuts*, I thought. *How can anyone do that?* But despite what I said, I knew Ashley would do it – he was a man on a mission.

Seeing Ashley training so hard had inspired me. I wanted to regain my fitness, but I had anxiety about returning to the gym and having to see people and talk to strangers again. There was no way I could keep up with Ashley on a run or on a bike, so my brother offered to go out cycling with me. Me and Danny had spent a lot of time sitting around indoors together and people started asking if I was alright because I was nowhere to be seen while Ashley was very visible around the town, riding his bike and pounding the pavements for hours on end. Danny and me started cycling down to Azaylia's Garden and it did us both the world of good to do something normal. Danny said he felt less stressed, and my head felt clearer. It was good to use my muscles again too. My grief was omnipresent, but ever so slowly, I began to feel slightly less numb inside.

. . .

I used to live in a very small world before Azaylia came along, I could see that now. My life revolved around me and Ashley and our loved ones and the rest of the world didn't really concern me but Azaylia had opened my eyes, shone her bright torch and showed me the bigger picture.

I was hearing all about other people's journeys with childhood cancers through my work with the foundation. Without exception, their stories were humbling, heartbreaking and incredibly inspiring. Helping these kids and their families was not just giving me a reason to get out of bed in the morning, it had become my passion and my life's work. I had more than a million followers on Instagram now and I was being asked to use my platform to promote products. I didn't hesitate. It was another gift from social media – the first one being my family of followers – because I not only enjoyed the work, but I could do it from home, leaving me plenty of time to devote to the foundation. I enjoyed earning a living again, and I found the work a good distraction, helping me cope with the waves of grief and anxiety I was experiencing.

● ● ●

I drove down to Land's End to support Ashley on the first leg of his bike challenge. The sun was just going down when they reached Newquay on 1 September 2021 and, very fittingly, the horizon was a strip of orange as he and his team raced along the seafront. Well-wishers were out in force, shouting, 'Let's go, champ!', which brought a lump to my throat. Azaylia's story had touched so many people – my little girl was *still* being amazingly inspirational, all these miles from home.

Before the bike ride, a couple had knocked on our door and told us they'd driven all the way from Lancashire to come and thank us for saving their marriage. Ashley and me were completely taken aback. 'How?' we asked. 'What do you mean?'

'We were on the verge of splitting up when we started to follow your story on social media,' the man said. 'It made us stop and think. It made us take stock of our lives and realise what we had to be thankful for.'

It blew us away, but that was how inspirational Azaylia was. We were custodians of her power now and I was so proud of the way we were representing her.

Ashley published the location of every finish line on his Instagram and the support he was receiving was phenomenal. He could hardly believe it. It was like a Mexican Wave of love spreading all the way from Land's End to John o' Groats, and it grew and grew as he and his team clocked up more miles. Hundreds of people started turning up to cheer them on at every checkpoint, come rain or shine and whatever the hour.

I love the fact that, however exhausted Ashley must have been, he took the time to speak to all the supporters and show his genuine appreciation: 'You guys are like a sea of energy, an army of love and spirit,' he shouted. 'Thank you so much!' It was wonderful to watch. Once again, we were seeing the faces behind the screens and it lifted the soul.

On 6 September I went with other family members to greet the team when they arrived on the banks of the River Trent in Nottingham. The place was rammed with supporters as far as the eye could see, all cheering and waving and holding orange balloons: 'We love you, Azaylia!' they yelled.

We went around with charity collection buckets, saying thank you to as many people as we could manage. I was bowled over. The love that was pouring from the crowd was incredible. Everywhere I turned people were telling me I was an amazing mummy and how Azaylia had made them appreciate their family more.

Ashley was fighting back the tears when he saw the turnout. He looked spent and, when I hugged him, I didn't want to let go. He still had more than half the journey to complete, but he wasn't complaining.

'I was physically and mentally exhausted after 407 miles of riding in the last 6 days,' he posted on Instagram later. 'Ahead of an 84-mile ride, in 29-degree heat with nearly 6,000 ft of climbing and I was feeling sorry for myself. I got weak before I realised that Azaylia and these incredible children battle through something far worse than this every single day. And I witnessed first-hand that not a day went by where she didn't smile, where she didn't fight and where she just sat there and felt sorry for herself. So why should I have that privilege? I will rise, I will battle and I will power through another day honouring her and all of these children fighting the good fight, for their lives!'

That said it all.

Ashley was on a spiritual journey too, he acknowledged. Pushing his physical boundaries was teaching him about himself and who he was. He'd been for a spiritual reading before embarking on the ride and the spiritualist had told him that Azaylia wanted him to start listening to music and dancing like he used to with her. It was the most important thing he took away from the reading, he said.

'So today we vibe, baby,' he smiled, posting a video online of him dancing to his music in his cycle gear. I grinned from ear to ear when I saw it – it was like watching a rainbow emerge from the clouds.

I'd also had a reading and, entirely unprompted, the spiritualist told me that Azaylia wanted to gift us a child. It was a heart-stopping moment, one I'll never forget. I would accept *anything* from Azaylia and I told the spiritualist I would love us to be a family again. I explained that I'd ruled out having another child because I felt so worried about how Azaylia would view it and I didn't want her to ever feel we tried to replace her. The woman told me that another baby would be an *addition* to our family, not a replacement, so there was nothing to feel guilty about. Similarly, if I wanted to move house or travel abroad or go away for work, I should do it. Azaylia would come with me wherever I went, just as she would have done if she had stayed on earth. It was such a relief to hear this and it made the future seem less bleak and uncertain.

· · ·

Azaylia was always going to have a brother or sister. That was our plan, right from the start. We didn't ever want her to be an only child and after the reading I dared to dream about whether she would gift us a girl or a boy – *I don't care*, I thought. *As long as the baby is happy and healthy and loved and protected, that is what counts.* We would teach him or her all about big sister Azaylia and what a hero she was. We weren't ready yet, but to know that Azaylia would support us if and when the time came was the most wonderful gift.

On 11 September 2021 Ashley crossed the border into Scotland and declared he was channelling his 'inner Azaylia', which really made me smile. He was embracing the challenge with all his heart and I was desperate to show him as much support as I could. I was weaving my way up north by car, driving for hours with my brother Danny, or with Ashley's mum Vicky, and stopping off at different checkpoints to give Ashley a hug and tell him how proud I was.

The team finally arrived at John o' Groats on 14 September 2021, having cycled an epic 1,070 miles in fourteen days. I never doubted that Ashley would do it – and within the extremely tough timeframe he set himself. Crowds had waited for hours, parents bringing kids in lion suits and orange tutus, all ready to give the biggest cheer.

It was cold and dark when I finally saw Ashley appear. He was sweating as he came up the hill and he looked physically and emotionally wiped out. A lone piper greeted the team home and the crowd of well-wishers went wild.

'We made it, baby!' Ashley said, looking up to the sky. 'We made it! Let's go, champ!'

My heart was dancing: our little girl had done this and I had so much pride and respect for her and her daddy.

*   *   *

It was my turn now to show Azaylia what I could achieve. After completing the bike ride, Ashley took on the 'Three Peaks', challenging himself not only to climb Ben Nevis, Scafell Pike and Snowdon – the highest mountains in Scotland, England and Wales – but also to cycle between them. We were only halfway through Children's Cancer Awareness month, he said, so why not squeeze in another fundraising event for the foundation?

He had already climbed to the summit of Ben Nevis and had cycled from there to the Lake District, where I joined him at Scafell Pike.

'Let's go!' I said bravely, the ice-cold air catching in my throat. Despite the fact that Ashley was much fitter than I was and could have done the climb a lot faster if he went off with his team, he was going to stay close to me the whole way, which I appreciated.

I thought about the fact that the old me would have shied away from a challenge like this. I'd have put it off until I'd done more training, or volunteered to raise funds some other way but I'd changed so much. Life is a struggle and this mountain was just the next challenge I had to face. I was so much stronger now, I had more patience and a drive and purpose in life I didn't possess before. I was going to show my daughter just how much she'd taught me and to help as many other little heroes as I could, however tough this was.

I had to keep reminding myself of all of those things as my legs started to burn, the rain became torrential, the wind tried to force me backwards and the bag on my back turned to stone. I felt so daunted and my emotions were rising closer and closer to the surface with every step I took. I stumbled and fell, I had agonising cramps, I was crying my eyes out … This was all too much, I thought. A nightmare that had to end, but it couldn't – I couldn't allow myself to think like that.

My head was pounding as I faced the final stretch. I wanted to click my fingers and make this all stop, but there was a voice on a loop going round and round in my head: *What would Azaylia do? What would Azaylia do? What would Azaylia do?*

I kept going, scanning the rocky path beneath my feet as I went. *It doesn't matter if you fall again*, I told myself, *you can pick yourself up, you've done it before.*

The final fifty-metre push felt like climbing another mountain in itself, but then I looked up and saw what I was searching for. There in the thick grey cloud and swirling mist was a patch of sky that was brighter than the rest.

It was Azaylia, waiting for me.

'I'm here!' I said, bursting into tears. 'I told you I'd do it, baby! Mummy made it!'

Ashley was there, just up ahead of me, and I broke down again when I looked into his eyes. They were tears of joy and exhilaration. We were all together at the top of the mountain, just as I told Azaylia we would be.

I wasn't in heaven, but I was a tiny step closer.

'I love you, Azaylia,' I said, looking high into the sky. 'We did it, baby.'

EPILOGUE

It's been almost a year since Azaylia passed. If you'd told me twelve months ago that I'd be sitting here now, putting the finishing touches to my book, I'd have said 'no way!', but life never fails to surprise me.

Reaching the top of Scafell Pike was a pivotal moment. I was at the highest point in England and I could choose where I wanted to go next: Azaylia had guided me that far and I looked to her again.

You're my hero, Azaylia. How can I be more like you?

Azaylia was kind and funny and big-hearted and inspirational. Not long after climbing the mountain, I was invited to attend the 2021 Pride of Britain awards ceremony in London. It was an incredibly important event for so many reasons. For a long time I felt I couldn't be seen to smile or dress in nice clothes for fear of what people who didn't know me might think or say. Would the public think I'd forgotten about Azaylia, or that

I wasn't grieving anymore? My confidence was so fragile and I didn't know how to rebuild it. But guess what? I got glammed up and I mingled with so many true heroes as well as celebrities, many of whom I grew up watching on TV. Sharon Stone, Rod Stewart, Simon Cowell and Joanna Lumley were there, along with the singer Ne-Yo, Molly-Mae Hague and Alesha Dixon, who was very supportive and chatted to me for a long time. I also met Peter Andre and his wife, Emily MacDonagh, who were there with their children. Emily had followed our journey and said she admired me for sharing Azaylia's story and would love to get involved in the foundation.

It was an eye-opening evening. Famous people were coming up to *me* and I didn't feel starstruck at all. That's because Azaylia is my hero, along with all the other children fighting fearlessly against cancer. Nobody else comes close. I realised I didn't have to be afraid or hide away: I was proud of my daughter and proud of myself, and that was really all that mattered.

My life now is all about aspiring to mirror Azaylia's amazing qualities as I continue to represent her through her foundation. Watching it grow is like watching my daughter grow up, and we've had a flying start. The Azaylia Foundation has already donated funds to support twelve-year-old 'Gorgeous George' having specialist treatment abroad for a rare brain tumour. We've helped seven-year-old Alexander have treatment in the UK and Germany to tackle his brain and spinal tumours. We donated funds to help Birmingham Children's Hospital buy equipment for augmented reality surgery, which has the potential to revolutionise surgical care for children with cancer. And we donated £120,000 to the University of Birmingham to fund a cell sorter machine, which helps provide detailed studies of how cancer cells respond to different treatments. These are just a few examples of the work we are doing with the foundation and it is only the beginning, because there are so many more exciting things to come.

At Christmas 2021 me and Ashley went shopping for toys and delivered them by the trolley-load to Birmingham Children's Hospital. Ashley's epic bike ride has raised almost £100,000 and he has more ambitious fundraising challenges ahead: 'I'm not scared about death any more,' he says. 'I'm scared about not doing enough while I'm here, to earn my place in heaven with Azaylia.'

I'm with him on that 100 per cent. Club 100 exists only in our heads nowadays, but its door is firmly open again and we will continue to work tirelessly, with love and positivity in our hearts, to help as many children with cancer as we possibly can. All of this is thanks to our truly inspirational daughter Azaylia Diamond Cain. You are our hero, baby, and we will love you forever and always, with all of our hearts.

You grew inside me, Azaylia, and from the moment your life began you made a giant imprint on my heart. Our bond is, and always will be, unbreakable.

Until we meet again in heaven,
let's go, champ! x

ACKNOWLEDGEMENTS

Thank you to Azaylia, my hero. You made me a mummy and gave me a million beautiful memories that I will treasure forever. You transformed me into the woman I am today, teaching me everything I needed to know in order to continue your legacy and earn my place with you in heaven. It has been an honour and a privilege to create the Azaylia Foundation and work in your name to help children and families fight fearlessly against childhood cancer.

Thank you to Ashley for standing by my side and being the most incredible father to Azaylia. I could not have asked for a more positive and resilient partner, and Azaylia is lucky to have you as her daddy.

My brother Danny, who has been there for me every step of the way and continues to be my rock. I will never be able to thank you enough.

The family and friends who have supported Ashley and me daily, and still do. You all know who you are. You loved Azaylia and you supported us emotionally and physically through the toughest times. You made us food, put our needs first and nourished us endlessly with your thoughtfulness and kindness.

A massive thank you to all our social media followers and the public for giving us an army of support and showing so much love to Azaylia. My Instagram followers are like a huge family around me now and I owe each and every one of you a huge debt of gratitude.

Writer Rachel Murphy for being so kind and sensitive in helping me write my book the way I wanted it.

Finally, a big thank you to Lydia Ramah and her fantastic team at Ebury Spotlight for allowing me to share my journey with everyone and raise awareness of childhood cancer. Your vision has made this happen.